THE COMPLETE

Explains everything there is to know about raw juices and how they can be used to aid recovery from a number of ailments and conditions, as well as to maintain health and vitality.

THE COMPLETE RAW JUICE THERAPY

by

SUSAN E. CHARMINE

NATURE'S WAY

THORSONS PUBLISHING GROUP
Wellingborough, Northamptonshire

Rochester, Vermont

First published 1977
First published in *Nature's Way* series 1981
Second Impression 1982
Third Impression 1983
Fourth Impression 1985
Fifth Impression 1987

British Library Cataloguing in Publication Data

Charmine, Susan E.
    The complete raw juice therapy.
    1. Fruit juices — Therapeutic use
    2. Vegetable juices — Therapeutic use
    I. Title
    615'.32   RM237.5

    ISBN 0-7225-0732-1

Printed and bound in Great Britain

CONTENTS

CHAPTER 1

HOW RAW JUICE THERAPY WORKS

Tragedies like the thalidomide affair are certain to recur for as long as the science and art of medicine continue to be developed. There is no way in which every possible individual side effect can be observed until a remedy has been used by great numbers of people over many years.

This is exactly the situation with herbal medicines and with the fruits and vegetables that we eat every day – not all herbs are good for you, and many fruits and vegetables are poisonous. The difference, though, is that mankind has already spent countless years testing food and trying nature's medicine chest of herbs so that the inevitable tragedies resulting from sampling the attractive-looking black fruits of deadly nightshade, or trying a feast of the death cap toadstool were discovered thousands of years before we were born. Even so, deadly nightshade (or, as the practitioner calls it, *belladonna*) in minute doses is helpful for colic or spasms. Our forefathers became very expert in their use of plants!

When raw juices are unlocked from the cells of plants, pure and vital liquids of great healing power are released, and their infinitely gentle action can coax our bodies back to normality. Raw juices have none of the potentially dangerous side-effects of many potent drugs, yet they can eliminate health problems arising from many of those deficiencies created by the bustle and pace of modern life.

The regular addition of such juices to a wise diet is also a great strengthener of bodily function, assisting in the prevention of the premature degeneration of skin, flesh, glands and organs that causes so many who should be enjoying a long and active prime of life to lapse into early senility.

For effective therapy you need to know which fresh

vegetable and fruit juices are needed to benefit the body. This book will explain the best for each condition, with the most important points of each therapy and the best ways of extracting the precious juices, both mechanically and by hand.

Sunshine and good healthy soil enlivened with refreshing rain allow plants to develop to a rich maturity, and the raw juices they yield are the quintessence of nature's handiwork. Readily available and easy to digest, they contain all the nutritional factors needed to supplement the diet. The ancient Romans knew this when they added honey, crushed or juiced fruits, aromatic plants and scented flowers to their drinks.

When used swiftly after extraction, raw fruit and vegetable juices are an incomparably effective way of rapidly utilizing the powers of the plants to protect you from illness. The composition of juices is so complex that analytical procedures give only a part of the truth. In addition it is not only the compositions of the individual juices which create their profound effects, it is the subtle natural balance between the constituent parts.

On the face of it juices do not seem likely to be very energizing, but, as Dr Valnet points out, the calorie content of a litre of grape or pineapple juice is between eight and nine hundred. To achieve the same you would need 1½ litres of milk or a dozen eggs, 3 pounds of potatoes or 650 grammes of meat. Apple juice contains 500 calories per litre; pear juice 420; cherry juice 450; orange juice 400; strawberry juice 220.

THE IMPORTANCE OF FRESHNESS

As soon as a fruit or vegetable is harvested it begins to deteriorate. But the deterioration during a reasonable period after gathering is as nothing when compared to the far greater losses experienced during even the most careful cooking. You have only to sample average restaurant cooking to be convinced that there exists a conspiracy between chef and waiter to deprive the customers of their nutritional entitlement! However, for the worst examples of boiled-to-death and kept-hot-for-ages food it is necessary to eat in a hospital, a school or a residence for the elderly. This is why it is essential to conserve *all* the advantages nature has provided by taking juices raw and fresh.

The body is being continuously renewed and re-vitalized. Every second that passes sees the renewal of millions of cells out of the total of almost 30 billion that go to make a man. This never-ceasing re-creation depends for success upon correct nutrition – not only with the three basic classes of foods, proteins, carbohydrates and fats, but also with vitamins, minerals and roughage.

The effects of extreme deprivation of vital food elements are appalling. The bloated belly of children suffering from protein deficiency is often seen in famine relief posters, less obvious is the greying hair, fever and skin sores. A lack of vitamin D causes the bent bones of rickets; of vitamin B1, beri-beri; of niacin, pellagra and of vitamin C, scurvy. There are recommended daily allowances of nutritional factors (which vary a good deal from country to country) that are sufficient to prevent any obvious deficiency. But is that good enough? For many the way to real health and vitality lies in the generous provision of these valuable substances so that the renewal of cells is not reduced in quality through even the slightest shortage.

Within a quarter of an hour of consumption on an empty stomach raw juices begin to enter the blood-stream through the digestive processes. Thus glands, organs and indeed every cell of the body are able to extract quickly their individual food requirements, enabling them to perform their functions in a strong and normal way, free from deprivation.

There is a sheer physical difficulty in simply eating the fresh fruit and vegetables in sufficient quantities to provide a therapeutic effect. It is possible to eat only limited amounts daily of the whole material, but once the juices have been released they are delicious and can be taken in sufficiency so that results are assured.

It is unwise to expect dramatic results from any natural treatment for a natural cure is, like the deterioration which brought about the condition in the first place, a long process. Patience is needed to undo the misuses of years. The complaints of middle age, even after years of evident good health, are hardly ever sudden occurences. They have been building up unseen and unfelt.

DETOXIFICATION OF THE SYSTEM

Nature cure depends for effectiveness on elimination of the toxic substances causing the condition, whereas the more dramatic results of the orthodox physician are more concerned with the suppression of the symptoms. For conditions which have appeared to become serious, self-diagnosis can lead to errors. There is really no substitute for the objective opinion of a trained and experienced practitioner, but the great advantage of raw juice therapy is that it is not normally made less effective when combined with other treatments.

An elimination of the toxic substances in the tissues begins with the therapy. The strength of this activity can develop and grow so that the wastes that have accumulated are first of all loosened and then mobilized. They are absorbed again by the blood-stream and afterwards excreted. This often causes an aggravation of the symptoms, or sometimes colds or boils or digestive upsets. In the young and vigorous this healing crisis may take place in the first six weeks of treatment, older or weaker people, especially when a chronic illness is present, often have no crisis at all. Or when they do it may be delayed for many months and be quite mild as the toxic material is disposed of slowly.

The pioneers of modern nature cure, such as Father Sebastian Kneipp, Preissnitz, Schroth, Dr J.H. Kellogg and Dr Henry Lindlahr, used the simplest methods to achieve their strikingly effective results. To the curative properties of air, water, earth and sunlight, the natural elements, they added the healing forces of plants. They saw disease as the *outcome* of a poor bodily and mental state where germs could flourish. Killing the germs is not a cure – for that you must so improve body and mind that there is no place the germ can develop.

Today advertising encourages the mother to use baby foods so that the natural protection and immunity which is the child's birthright and comes from breast feeding is denied. As a distinguished British paediatrician said: 'I simply cannot see why all normal mothers do not breast feed, for not only is the mixture just right, it is more healthy, free of charge, at the correct temperature, there when you need it and beautifully packed.'

In these days of convenience foods it is refreshing to read Father Kneipp's practical and down-to-earth nutritional comments for the less well off. They could equally well apply to the excellent eating ideas of many young people today who are bringing about a resurgence of healthy eating in their homes and communes. Kneipp wrote in *Thus Shalt Thou Live* in 1889:

> 'I will mention a poor married couple who were blessed with thirteen children and found it very hard to provide food for them. Every morning the children had a somewhat thick soup such as brown peasant bread soup, potato soup, cooked flour soup with potatoes or a sort of porridge made with potatoes and meal. Such a meal was greatly relished by the healthy, vigorous children. In the middle of the morning when hunger set in again they would have potatoes and bread, or when there was milk in the house, bread and milk.
>
> For dinner they had some strong soup, steamed meal and milk. In the afternoon some brown bread, and if milk were added they were supremely happy. In the evening bread soup was again placed on the table with a draught of milk if there was any. You would not easily have found a family that could show healthier or stronger children!
>
> Do not be afraid lest their food be too rough and plain. I knew a mother who used to have rye, barley and oats ground and the whole baked with the bran as bread for her children. They were capitally fed. By giving your children white bread or dishes prepared from refined flour you are giving them poor nourishment.'

The same philosophy is so very true of raw juice therapy. Nature is complete and whole – we must extract the whole of the juice from the fruit or vegetable in the same way as we should use the whole of the grain in our cooking.

So natural cures necessitate moving away from the sophisticated and refined, partially synthetic foods that are everywhere about us, back to those living cells which are composed of the same organic building blocks as comprise all living things. If you think this may not make for an exciting cuisine, I am glad to say that you are mistaken, for imaginatively prepared pure foods can be both complex and sublime. In any case you may take consolation from that brilliant composer, mystic and natural therapist Cyril Scott who, taking a cake from the tray in his ninety-first year said to me, 'So long as you eat enough of the proper foods, the body can well take care of the occasional indiscretion!'

Nevertheless, an abrupt change from a bad diet of long duration to a therapeutic diet with raw juices is very definitely not going to agree with the digestions of the majority. You will find wind disturbing your tranquillity, and sometimes diarrhoea your peace of mind (King George III was so afflicted by this complaint that he took his own portable closet with him on all State occasions. He called the condition 'merrygowhimbles'.) Be reassured that these reactions do not mean a failure or an incompatability with the treatment. They are simply part of the detoxification process during which the body has to make many adjustments on the road back to health.

RAPID CHANGE IN EATING HABITS

The human body evolved to its present high state of perfection through becoming adapted to the natural foods selected as good for it. In terms of evolutionary time the rapid transition we have made in our eating habits in these last hundred years has left us unable to adapt. The result is that, when you take the mortality rates of those who have already reached middle age and are therefore past the crises of childhood, you see only a small gain in this last century when the great advances in medicine and hygiene should have been far more rewarding. We are not giving ourselves perfect food. We are not giving ourselves a fair chance of survival. The best, most perfect food is prepared by nature and selected by man.

Sparkling health comes when our bodies are free from toxins and able to rebuild the cellular structure from first class nutrient materials. Recently the cereal fibre or roughage advocated by Kneipp in Germany, Allinson in Britain and Kellogg in the U.S.A., all before 1900, has become medically recognized after three-quarters of a century of scorn. When will it be realized that the alternatives to powerful drugs and to denatured foods are also part of the heritage of man; a part that has somehow got lost on the way forward; a part that sensible and practical people are daily rediscovering for themselves.

Do not ignore the strength of the mind. To brood on an affliction is to aggravate it. Worry makes us tired and depressed to start with, and then can leave us prone to illness, without resistance. Physicians rarely catch the diseases of their patients because they have a positive mental attitude which excludes this possibility. However, the stress and often inadequate diet that can be part of the practitioner's life makes him an above average risk from heart conditions. More and more are giving up smoking, cutting down on refined sugar and turning to vegetable oils. No doubt they will get round to raw juices before long, but you can make a start today.

A friend spent several of his war years as a prisoner of the Japanese. The living conditions were incredibly hard, and many died from fever or from malnutrition. Frank was skilled in his knowledge of plants. By growing yeasts for vitamin B and protein, and by making juice drinks from wild plants he not only survived even the rigours of the building of the bridge over the River Kwai, he saved many of his colleagues as well.

Scurvy was for thousands of years the scourge of sailors and soldiers on expeditions. In 1593 Admiral Sir Richard Hawkins wrote of 10,000 seamen having died from scurvy in his personal experience. The first effective juice therapy for scurvy seems to have been during Jacques Cartier's second voyage to Newfoundland in 1535 when the disease was killing many of his crew. One sailor learnt that the Red Indians made an extract from the needles of spruce trees as a remedy. They tried it with apparently miraculous results as all the sailors recovered rapidly.

Admiral Hawkins was using lemon juice to good effect by 1593 and by 1617 John Woodall was writing in his book *The Surgeon's Mate*: 'The use of the juice of Lemmons is a precious medicine and well tried, being sound and good …. In want whereof use the juice of limes or oranges, citrons, or the pulp of tamarinds.' To achieve the results there must have been experiments with many different juices. It is salutary to note that the first breakthrough came by following the medical practices of a so-called primitive tribe. What had really happened was that civilization had eroded man's ability to live at one with his environment. He had to learn again the skills of his ancestors who were familiar with the valuable properties of juices.

Why do the juices work best when raw? The answer lies in the destructibility through heat of the enzymes. Enzymes are produced by living cells to allow all the thousands of reactions that need to take place to occur rapidly so that the cells can function. Enzymes are proteins like egg white, which is also protein, they are destroyed by temperatures over 130°F.

Enzymes are sensitive to change (observe the rapid browning of a cut apple exposed to the air) but survive freezing. Indeed the enzymes present in the mammoth flesh found in Siberian glaciers are active 50,000 years after some catastrophe engulfed the massive beasts in ice.

The aim of raw juice therapy is to make all the valuable elements available and easy to assimilate so that they can work to revitalize the whole system. They are so easy to digest that old people can take them as easily as their children and grandchildren. Raw juices also help to control appetite so that the regular juice taker finds it easier to maintain or regain a healthy weight.

There are two vitamins which the body can store and does not eliminate when taken to excess. These are vitamins A and D. Our bodies can produce vitamin A from carrot juice, but the quantities recommended in this book will do no harm. In 1975 there was an extreme case of a London man who lived on carrot juice supplemented with vitamin A tablets. He went yellow all over but would not stop his gigantic intake of vitamin A. Sad to say, he died. The press wrote 'Health Addict Dies', but that man was no more a health addict than is an alcoholic. Raw juice therapy is a safe and natural way to health. Let us, in the next chapter, look at some case histories.

CHAPTER 2

RAW JUICE THERAPY IN ACTION

The orthodox medical practitioner when confronted with one of nature's therapies is often frankly sceptical, or even downright abusive. He will say that case histories are not the sort of proof that he can accept. And he is quite right! Doctors in the future will look back on the last half of the twentieth century as an age in which the patient became the slave to science instead of science existing to serve the patient.

This is why. In order to *prove* that a medicine is effective it is necessary to carry out what is called a double blind trial. To do this a large number of patients showing similar characteristics and having the same complaint are divided randomly into two groups. Their doctors are given the new medicine, only this is also provided in two similar looking batches. One batch contains the medicine, the other does not.

This means that neither doctor nor patient can tell who is having the treatment and who is not. Only the research team knows the truth. The results are analysed by statisticians and the effectiveness of the medicine judged. At the same time the side effects are catalogued and the decision made as to whether the adverse reactions observed so far, outweigh the benefits or not.

In this way a very accurate estimation can be made to *prove*, beyond any reasonable doubt whether or not the medicine works and is safe. Like thalidomide! But, to be fair, many therapeutic advances have been made by these means. The awful medical mistake is to go on from there to reject out of hand therapies that are not able to be tested in this way.

Nature Cure starts from the idea that the whole person and the whole organism should be treated as a unit. As Kneipp says, when writing of the treatment of chronic

open sores on the feet, 'It is quite inconceivable to me
that people do not believe that the cause of an open foot
sore is a diseased body, and that to heal the feet the body
must be treated. This healing can only take place when all
foul matter in the body is dispersed and expelled and the
system braced and strengthened to resist the admission of
foul matter within it.

This is the only natural cure. Nothing should be done to
the feet themselves beyond keeping them clean.'

In the year 1893 Father Kneipp treated over 12,000
patients at his Kurhaus in the little German village of
Wörishofen. This healing establishment was run by the
Brothers and Sisters of Charity. There is still today a very
active Kneipp Society in Germany.

Yet this sort of treatment, with its wonderful results for
patients who had been given up as beyond help, cannot
be tested with the double blind (or the more complex
triple blind) trial and so is not acceptable to many of
today's doctors. Men who so frequently treat just the
symptoms and not the causes of disease.

The British Minister of Health has said that Britain does
not have, as commonly supposed, the best State health
service there is, but the best disease service. He has called
for a greater awareness of the importance of preventative
medicine. Father Kneipp would have applauded him! He
would even be able to tell him that for success he would
have to start the prevention with publicity for a healthy,
natural diet.

The Complete Book of Food and Nutrition by J.I.
Rodale, in a mostly favourable discussion on the book
Raw Juice Therapy by J.H. Lust, calls the author to task for
advocating specified blends of different juices for various
complaints. In fact Lust, and many other natural healers
for the last two thousand recorded years, recommend on
the basis not only of their own experience but on the
findings of other therapists that have stood the dual tests
of safety and effectiveness for very many years.

GOOD, SAFE AND WELL-TRIED
This book does not pretend that raw juices are the sole
form of therapy, but simply that they are good, safe, well-

tried and have returned many to health. Raw juices are also delicious and a splendid pick-me-up against strain and weariness.

How much then do these valuable juices, the vital extractions of nature's plant kingdom, benefit the ill?

John B. Lust reports the case of Mr. P.O'-, from Wisconsin. At the time he wrote, this man was 61 and had been enjoying good health for seven years. He had become ill with bladder trouble at the age of 25. By the time he was 40 this had progressed to the stage where he suffered from pain, burning sensations, frequent urination and bleeding.

Drug treatment proved of no avail. With the diagnosis of a tumour on the prostate, possibly cancerous, he was advised to undergo surgery. At 50 he was thinking of suicide, but he read that the ideal diet was raw food. He reasoned that raw juices would be an efficient way of consuming a lot of raw food. As his gums were tender from pyorrhoea, which is pus in the sockets of the teeth, the ease of raw juice therapy was particularly appealing.

After a three day fast during which hot, moist packs were applied to the areas of the teeth and the bladder, he began to take the fresh juices. These were a mixture of apple, orange, spinach, carrot, beet, celery, cucumber and parsley juices.

He soon grew in strength and was comforted. During the next two years he gradually transformed his diet so that all his solid foods were raw fruits and vegetables. Mild herbal laxatives were taken for constipation (this writer would have preferred the use of wheat bran and molasses).

Toxins were dispersed through all the eliminative organs, including the skin. He looked yellowed, lost much weight and felt unwell and unhappy because of the eliminative processes. But at the end of this prolonged healing crisis his feeling of well-being rapidly returned and his weight and appetite became normal.

After that the gradual process of recovery went steadily ahead. Stamina and strength developed with firmer muscles and more effective organs. There had been a complete cure of his bladder and prostate conditions.

The cure would have been much faster if the treatment had been undertaken before the body had deteriorated so much. It illustrates, though, that there is hope even for the most chronically ill, so do not give in to disease – fight it hard.

ALFRED McCANN

A pioneer publicist for the common sense of a healthy diet was the New York journalist and author Alfred McCann. It seems that it was McCann himself who saved the crew of the German cruiser *Kronprinz Wilhelm*.

This ship was forced into the navy base of Newport News on 11 April 1915 after being at sea for 255 days. There was gross malnutrition amongst the crew. Fifty could not stand up and more were dropping out at the rate of two per day. The health of the whole crew was disintegrating and the morale was very low.

The symptoms included atrophy of the muscles, dilated heart, paralysis and anaemia. The Captain knew that he would be responsible for a crew of five hundred dead men unless a cure was found. So he made for the nearest port in the James river. McCann tells us that here was a crew of men living in the open air, eating the staple articles of diet, namely: fresh meat, all the fat and dairy products they wanted, boiled potatoes canned vegetables, sugar, tons of fancy cakes, biscuits and white bread, and all the tea and coffee they could drink.

These German sailors were eating a typical 'civilized' diet. The sort of nourishing food many mothers give their families with the single exception that the average family would *add fresh fruit and vegetables*. And this would be enough to avoid the striking condition suffered by the sailors.

McCann suggested the remedy after the doctors on shore had failed. He thought it was necessary to provide more 'food salts'. Now it would be seen that he was using a form of natural vitamin therapy. On 15 April they began the road to recovery.

To 100lbs of wheat bran was added 200lbs of water. The mixture was left for twelve hours at 120°F. The liquor was drained off and 8oz. given to each man every morning.

Each man also received one teaspoonful of wheat bran morning and night. Cabbages, carrots, parsnips, spinach, onions and turnips were boiled together for two hours. The liquid was drained off and used in generous portions as soup with unbuttered wholemeal bread. The residue was discarded.

They washed and peeled potatoes, threw away the potatoes and kept the skins! These were boiled in water, and after straining off the liquid the men were given 4oz. a day of the liquid.

The final items of the diet were milk and fresh fruit juice. It took only ten days for 47 out of the most seriously ill to be cured, according to the ship's doctor. Shortly afterwards the entire crew was fit enough to return to sea. It is to be hoped that they had learned their lesson. Perhaps this case is one of the most significant large-scale tests of fruit and vegetable juices on record. It is certainly compelling evidence of the value of the therapy.

Alfred McCann also reports a smaller scale but no less interesting experiment on twelve convicts in a Mississippi jail. Six of the men were murderers and all were serving long sentences. The governor offered them a pardon if they would live for a number of weeks on an experimental diet.

The diet consisted of white biscuits, gravy, corn bread, grits, hominy, collard greens (a type of primitive cabbage that does not form a head), fried mush, polished rice, coffee and sugar.

This sounds not too bad for a sixty-day experiment, with freedom at the end. Yet after only a part of the test had taken place several of the men were in such pain from deficiency diseases that several had tried to kill themselves. Two, Guy R. James and D.W. Pitts applied to the penitentiary board to be sent back to their cells to resume their life sentences.

The men were suffering from pellagra which is caused by a deficiency of the vitamin called niacin, and from mineral shortages. The test was ended and the men quickly restored to health by means of a properly balanced diet.

These examples show the great value that can result

from the wise use of juices in combination with a sensible way of eating. It is one of mankind's responsibilities to his creator to be as healthy as he is able. In this way he can make the best contribution to life and society and to the family of man.

In the right circumstances nature is a great healing force. The minerals, trace elements and vitamins so generously provided in raw juices allow the powerful recuperative qualities of the body to take effect in an ideal and gentle manner. The cells are nourished and health is restored.

EVERYDAY CASE HISTORIES

It is dramatic to write of cures for very serious diseases through the effects of simple medicines. Indeed, there are many such cases on record and they show beyond doubt that the word 'hopeless' should never be used whilst life continues. But here you can read of some of those results with raw juices where success has been achieved at a more everyday level.

Simon S. of Stockport has suffered from severe sinus trouble for many years. As a schoolteacher he found his painful and tiring condition was seriously affecting his work. Not only did he find it hard to concentrate, he became more and more intolerant of his pupils and their foibles. Drugs sometimes brought relief, but this was always of short duration. His wife was in despair until she heard of a natural practitioner nearby who had helped many people.

For her, the most difficult part of the treatment was the task of convincing her husband to go and see him. After the first visit the practitioner asked to see the wife as well. He explained that although the man of the house was the sufferer, the problem was adversely affected by the food they ate. They were told to cut down on their con-sumption of milk, sugar and all starchy things with the exception of some daily whole grain in the form of cereal or bread.

Vegetables were to be raw or lightly cooked, and fresh fruit was to replace the cream cakes in their diet. They were to invest in an electric juicer. This became one of the finest bargains of their lives, for with it Simon was able to have daily supplies of the nutrients which, in the course of the next seven months, restored his health.

As a natural disinfectant, he was told to take 3 garlic capsules twice a day (if you juice your own garlic, then the machine is virtually useless for other purposes for a week, so buy capsules which are in any case odourless). Three times a day, after meals, he took a bare half teaspoonful of freshly grated horseradish blended with lemon juice (this mixture keeps for about a week).

In the morning Simon took 10 fl.oz. (275ml) of carrot juice mixed with 4 fl. oz. (100ml) of cucumber juice. In the evening he had another 10 fl.oz. (275ml) of the carrot, but this time with 5 fl.oz. (150ml) of radish juice made from both root and leaves. When cucumbers and radishes were not available he was allowed to substitute with spinach juice.

When Simon was able to pronounce himself 'cured', his practitioner warned him that he was not, nor would ever likely to be cured in the sense that he could revert with impunity to his old eating habits. He must continue to be careful. Simon assured that there was no fear of his relaxing his diet. When asked why that was, he said that his wife was now so radiant and well that she now knew true health for the first time – and to crown everything with joy, they were now expecting their first child!

Joseph L., an accountant living in one of the more exclusive North London suburbs, was heavily overweight. Like so many elderly Jewish people of his generation, he ate well of the delights that had comforted his well-off Eastern European childhood. A year in a concentration camp had left a scar on his mind which indulgence and hard work pushed to the background. He suffered a slight heart attack, Joseph was sent to hospital for a week or two and given the usual correct and wise advice that heart patients are asked to follow.

He was to reduce weight, take regular gentle exercise, cut down animal fats in favour of vegetable oils, stop smoking, and so on. He was scared, scared that he could not follow the advice, scared he would die before his time. His appetite was huge but his love of food made him see the fallacy of trying to replace real food by those synthetic disasters which so often hid under the term 'diet food' and were never what nature knew about.

Joseph struggled for a month or two but, though a man of tenacity, he failed to lose more than a couple of pounds and, what is more, he felt miserable about that! Then, in his search for a solution, he visited a health store. The owner was knowledgeable and had a long talk with his customer. Some books were suggested, some whole and natural foods were sold – and Joseph also asked the store owner to deliver a juicer to his house that day.

Joseph had quickly grasped the idea that naturally complete foods are more filling than their calorie equivalent of processed foods. He had noted in a magazine that raw juices helped people slim. He was ready to try it out. First of all he read his books and studied the magazine article, then he planned his weight reduction programme.

He learnt that rapid weight reduction could be harmful and that the *occasional* excess was not the end of the world. He found that a breakfast of citrus juice with a slice of wholewheat bread and vegetable margarine, was a positive help to slimming. This way you can miss that mid-morning break, or confine it to a little juice. Lunch was a mixed raw salad with perhaps a little cottage cheese. In the evening, some beans, or a little meat or fish without fat, and another salad.

By all accounts and on past history, Joseph should have been starving, but he was satisfied. This is because he complemented his diet with a freshly prepared raw juice cocktail before every meal. He made a fresh supply each evening which he stored in the refrigerator for the next day. This was his mixture: 10 fl.oz. (275ml) carrot juice; 1 whole juiced lemon; 5 fl.oz. (150ml) cucumber juice, plus, as available, the juice of a handful each of spinach, watercress, celery and parsley (at least one each time but as many as he had).

Joseph was still alive and well in his eighties, more than twenty years after his warning heart attack, and still with a zest for life. Neighbours look on him as that slim, upright and vigorous old man who is forever helping local charities with their accounting problems.

NERVOUS IRRITABILITY

Elizabeth R. lived on a farm in a small Suffolk village. She had an adoring husband and three lovely children. It was a smallish farm and, although they worked hard long hours, they never seemed to have quite enough money. The children were becoming expensive as they grew older. Elizabeth lost her tranquillity, and she became nervous and irritable.

The doctor, who had known her from childhood, was sympathetic. She was told to take it easy and was put on a course of tranquillizers. At first she improved but then, as she became accustomed to the drugs and as their toxic effects began to build up in her tissues, the old nerviness began to come back again, destroying the happy home atmosphere.

This time her husband, who was a man born of the soil and who had seen the harmful effects of some drugs on his animals, would not let her go on taking barbiturates. A few days before at the five hundred year old local inn, he had been talking to a German doctor of medicine. He was surprised to learn that about one doctor in ten in that country has done additional studies in natural medicine. The young farmer begged him to come and see his wife. The German agreed, provided the patient's own doctor was also present. Like so many country doctors, Elizabeth's had an enquiring nature and, in spite of his training, an open mind. He willingly assented and together they made the examination.

When someone is 'nervy' there does not appear to be all that much to see, but the German pointed out loss of elasticity in the skin, dull eyes with unclear whites, speckles of white on the finger nails, lack-lustre hair and many other small but significant points. These led him to believe that mineral deficiencies had so weakened Elizabeth's general powers of resistance to stress that she could not cope with the normal strain of a busy life.

To the amazement of the English doctor, his Continental colleague prescribed juices. First of all the juice of melissa mixed with the juice of what he called Johanniskraut. They worked out that this meant St John's herb, and from there they checked and found that the botanical name was *Hypericum perforatum* and was St John's wort in English. They also found that melissa was balm or lemon balm. They managed to borrow a juicer, found the herbs and extracted the juices.

Two teaspoonsful four times a day began to produce a calming effect on the nervous system without toxic side effects. At the same time to provide the minerals needed to overcome the deficiency (probably caused by too much care for others and too little for herself) she took 10 fl.oz. (175ml) of carrot juice with 5 fl.oz. (150ml) of raw red beet juice in the morning. Before going to bed she had a further 10 fl.oz. (275ml) of carrot together with 6 fl.oz. (175ml) of that valuable nerve tonic celery juice, plus 2 fl.oz. (50ml) each of parsely and spinach juice. You may think a pint is a lot in the evening, but it may be sipped slowly over the period of an hour or two if so wished.

A gradual process of cleansing and strengthening took place in Elizabeth's nervous tissues and bodily systems so that after three months she was her normal self again. She still had to deal with the very real and unavoidable worries that were a part of her life, but the difference was that she was now able to attack the problems instead of allowing the problems to attack her. The children are now old enough to help out after school and at weekends. Things are picking up and they are happy and fulfilled.

Fred was nine years old when he broke his leg at the thigh falling from his bicycle. The hospital set the fracture beautifully and within a couple of weeks he was collecting the signatures of his friends on the plaster cast. But it still hurt and when Fred went for a check up the bones were not knitting together as they should.

His godfather was a natural practitioner and when he heard of the trouble he checked up and found that since the accident the indulgent parents had given Fred lots of puddings and sweet things 'for the energy' and not much else. Paul pointed out that any fracture, burn or severe injury means a great surge in the body's need for protein, vitamins and minerals – especially vitamin C.

So Fred had a quick dietary change. Plenty of protein, milk, for the calcium, citrus fruits and fresh green vegetables for the vitamin C and the minerals. Then, to drink in the morning, 10 fl.oz. (275ml) carrot juice with 6 fl.oz. (175ml) celery juice; at lunchtime, 5 fl.oz. (150ml) carrot juice, 4 fl.oz. (100ml) beet and 1 fl.oz. (25ml) parsley juice; in the evening 5 fl.oz. (150ml) carrot juice, and 5 fl.oz. (150ml) orange juice.

Two weeks later at the next check-up, the hospital doctor was delighted at the rapid healing that a change in diet had brought about. By the way, Fred thereafter drank unsweetened juices for pleasure and avoided the sugary drinks of his friends. His teeth are good and his general fitness superb.

These case histories make it clear that the human individual has to be looked at as a whole. It is no good treating the symptoms whilst neglecting those basic deficiencies that prevent the healing powers of the body from acting in the powerful way intended by nature.

Few people go through life without illness. Remember that for any cure to have a chance, the basic nutrition of the body must be supplied in an assimilable form. For old people who have difficulty in eating enough of the right foods, raw juices should be taken as a supplement rather than as a remedy (unless there is illness). A routine glass of carrot juice mixed with orange with perhaps a touch of celery will aid vitality and resistance.

CHAPTER 3

DIETARY WISDOM – WHAT FOOD DOES AND IS

The next chapter is devoted to an analysis of the most important fruits and vegetables used in raw juice therapy. Nutritional terms are bandied about with much enthusiasm and little learning in the popular press. It is therefore a good idea to know something about nutrition so that you can understand the merits of the various foods we eat, and create your own balanced diet.

CARBOHYDRATES

The carbohydrates are the starches and sugars which are the main providers of energy for keeping the body working and coping with the activities we undertake. Western man has about half his diet in the form of carbohydrate but in the east it constitutes up to 90%, usually taken as grains. It is fortunate that grains are also good providers of protein, and starvation is generally the result of too little food rather than too few carbohydrates.

The refining of carbohydrates into white flour, polished rice and white sugar is a prime cause of overweight. Such foods are easy to eat in large amounts whereas if they are as near nature as possible – for example as wholewheat flour, brown rice and raw sugar – the appetite is well satisfied with less quantity.

Another bonus is that the all important roughage probably in its best form as cereal fibre (bran), is retained thus lessening the chance of the person who replaces his food with the natural alternative contracting of those diseases of western civilization that are of nutritional origin. These include diverticulitis, appendicitis and perhaps even varicose veins.

It must be remembered that brown bread is often coloured with caramel, and has added wheatgerm (a good food in itself), but is basically made from a refined or semi-refined flour. It is safest to insist when you can on bread from stoneground wholewheat flour as this will contain all the necessary nutrients.

FATS

The fats provide a concentrated store of energy in the body. Weight for weight they provide twice as much energy as do either carbohydrates or proteins. If you eat too much of any of these three basic food materials your body can store the surplus as fat.

A lot has been said about the advantages of vegetable fats over animal fats. This is to over-simplify the problem. The great change in the balance and quantity of fats in our diet this century has been away from the soft or polyunsaturated fats and towards the hard or saturated fats. Normally animal fats and dairy fats are saturated.

We are eating too much fat of *all* kinds and should reduce the quantity with ideally two thirds being polyunsaturated. These are found in grains and cereals especially soya, maize or corn, sunflower, linseed, sesame and safflower. Some vegetable fats are quite as saturated as the animal variety, examples of these, which should be taken only in moderation are coconut and palm oils.

There is much evidence, and the majority of nutritionists would support the view, that too much fat in the diet, especially if it is saturated, increases the chance of arteriosclerosis and heart attacks, whilst a moderate consumption of the polyunsaturated fats together with some saturated positively reduces the amount of cholesterol in the blood and with it the chance of it being deposited upon the walls of the arteries. The same thinking goes into the recommendation that you should not eat an average of more than one egg a day because eggs are rich in cholesterol.

In an average Western diet, polyunsaturated fat accounts for about one fifth of the total fat consumption. For good health it would be desirable to increase this figure to around three fifths. To do this you can use soft margarines made with vegetable oils, and cook in the best oils such as corn or sunflower. If you eat meat, cut off the fat; and remember that cocoa butter is very saturated, so too much chocolate is not a good idea.

PROTEINS

You need protein for the repair and growth of the body. Protein is composed of chains of amino acids. There are only twenty different amino acids but they are combined in nature in an infinite number of ways so that proteins differ in structure and in their enzymatic qualities.

In the old days scientists spoke of first and second class proteins. Today we know that out of the twenty amino acids, eight are *essential* in that the adult cannot make them in the body, and the rest are called *non-essential* because they can be made from the essential ones. One more amino acid, histidine, is needed for growing infants, and so is essential to begin with, but not later on.

It is a mistake to think of the non-essential amino acids as being without value for they too are found in the cells of our bodies, it is only that we can do without them if we have to. The essential amino acids are: isoleucine, leucine, lysine, methionine, phenylalanine, threonine, tryptophan and valine.

Most vegetable sources of protein are lacking in one or other of the essential amino acids, but meats contain all the amino acids in the correct proportions. However, if you mix grains, seeds and legumes so that your diet is not consisting of a single type of vegetable protein, then the biological value of the mixture is perfectly adequate. Indeed such a diet is good because it does not contain the saturated fat commonly present in meat.

If you do not have enough energy-providing food then the protein is used to provide heat and energy instead of materials for the growth and repair of the cells. Only recently did the World Health Organization realize that vast sums were being spent on giving protein to the starving and under-privileged millions, when all the poor were doing was to convert the protein to much-needed energy. When energy providing foods are given instead the protein levels usually do not need supplementation.

MINERALS

Although most of the inorganic elements found in nature can be found in our bodies, only fifteen are known to be absolutely necessary. Another five or six are needed by various animals, and it may be that their functions in man will also be discovered in due course.

There are eight major minerals and seven trace elements. With the exceptions of calcium and phosphorus the amounts present in a normal man seem very low, and it can take many years for signs of deficiency to develop, so slow is their loss. All the same they are vital to life and all are present in raw juices.

A normal man's body when reduced to ashes will contain the following amounts of the main fifteen minerals:-

Major minerals	Body content
Calcium	1,000g
Chlorine	95g
Iron	4.2g
Magnesium	19g
Potassium	140g
Phosphorus	780g
Sodium	100g
Sulphur	140g

Trace elements	
Chromium	2mg
Cobalt	1.5mg
Copper	72mg
Fluorine	2.6g
Iodine	13mg
Manganese	12mg
Zinc	2.3g

VITAMINS

The vitamins are a group of chemically different organic compounds which are needed in minute quantities for the normal functioning of our bodies. They were only recognized in this century and it is fair to say that research into vitamins still has far to go. There is not even general agreement about which vitamins are necessary and in what amounts.

The important thing to remember is that only two vitamins, A and D can be taken to excess, and any harmful effects from these require huge amounts such as would not come from raw juices.

ENERGY AND OBESITY

Overweight is classified as a disease by some doctors, and there is no question about the un-beautiful sight of increasing numbers of fat men, women and children inhabiting the more prosperous parts of our planet.

What is overweight? Dr Pawan of London's Middlesex Hospital tells us that half the population of Britain is overweight and half of those, obese. Obesity, he tells us, is being ten per cent over the standard in the usual height/weight tables.

It is sad, but exercise does not do much to take weight off. However, regular exercise certainly contributes to general health and can improve shape and general appearance.

Your ideal body weight requires, then, energy to keep it going. If you are overweight your balanced diet should be reduced to somewhat below your needs so that you have to burn off the surplus as energy. People do not put on weight in a few days, they take years at it. Be wise and slim slowly. Take fruit and vegetable juices to soften the pangs of hunger and to provide essential nutrients.

CANCER – IS CONTROL IN SIGHT?

The man, whether he be an unorthodox or an orthodox practitioner, who promises a cure for cancer is not to be trusted. However, the rate of control, where the disease is conquered and is not seen to return, is ever increasing and constitutes a triumph of medicine. Indeed, some cancers are controlled with complete long term success in more than 90% of cases. Other forms are controlled only rarely, for cancer is not one condition but many.

Spontaneous cessation occurs from time to time, and it is difficult to decide if the treatment is effective unless it is subject to an extensive trial. Nevertheless, there are indications that a number of natural treatments are being used with good results. Some are not within the subject matter of this book but it is important to mention some of those that are.

A large series of post-mortem examinations at Lund in Sweden showed that, although 22% of the patients had died of cancers, another 22% had malignancies which had not caused them any apparent trouble. This, as Dr Nieper of Hanover writes, means that we must understand that there is not a sharp line dividing those who have cancer from those who do not. The success of a treatment is, in the long term, dependent upon the body's power to resist the disease even if it is there.

Surgery, chemotherapy and radiation treatments are thus by way of stop-gap measures. Chemotherapy works by being toxic to the cancer, and to the person in a lesser degree. Such treatments can bring long remissions and in the case of children with leukaemia, a hitherto undreamt of prolongation of life.

The ideal treatment must be without side effects so that the body can fight the cancer without the stress of also having to fight the treatment. This must remain true even when the treatment has to be continued for very many years. The man with the desire to live must be prepared to alter his life style to give him a chance of victory.

It is not advisable to reject orthodox treatments because their short term benefit can give the body much needed time and peace to take advantage of the powers of healing that can be stimulated in other ways. Hormone treatment has a place, and Dr Vester has indicated the positive results to be obtained from mistletoe. Dr Nieper recommends, after long research, that the diet should be high in acids (this is made much easier with citrus juices). No meat from animals that have been injected with hormones, especially battery chickens, and no shellfish or anchovies because of the high level of nuclein, should be eaten.

Food should be rich in nitrilosides which are found in many foods, the best being apricot kernels (20 a day is proposed), wild berries, apple pips and millet. You can juice whole apples including the pips to advantage. It is also important to eat foods that are rich in the proteolytic enzymes. Papaya juice is one of the best sources, and pineapple is also good. They must be fresh or frozen.

The New York Cancer Research Institute has records of remissions from taking carotene (pro vitamin A) alone. As mentioned in the notes on carrot juice, which is the best and most easily assimilated source, it should be mixed with milk or cream for the best absorption.

No one who has, or suspects he might have, cancer should ever delay taking skilled advice. The foregoing information is intended to guide the patient towards the use of natural treatment in support of that given by his practitioner. All the examples are taken from the modern work of properly qualified medical doctors from several countries but represent experiences which are not perhaps so well known as they should be. They do not conflict with other medicines or treatments and the practitioner should always be advised of what the patient is taking to help control his condition.

There is no question that a positive attitude enormously helps the body towards a remission which can well be permanent. This when coupled with appropriate changes in the diet has given thousands a new lease of life.

CHAPTER 4

THE COMPOSITION AND ANALYSIS OF RAW MATERIALS FOR JUICE THERAPY

The descriptions of plants and vegetables many times mention the wide variations found in their vitamin and mineral contents. What is sure is that storage and cooking are major factors in reducing what is present naturally. Therefore, raw fruits, vegetables and their juices are ideal ways of obtaining maximum nourishment.

The therapeutic uses of juices require that all the factors that are normally present are consumed in sufficient quantities to be efficacious. It would be impossible for most people to consume the amount of raw cabbage needed to give the pint or two a day needed for the treatment of a gastric ulcer. But it is not difficult to take the cabbage in the form of juice.

The use of the following tables will enable the reader to choose supplementary juices and foods to reinforce and intensify the actions of the juices recommended in the therapeutic index. Remember, juices are never dangerous. But, some drugs are so dangerous that the side effects are almost as bad as the condition they are supposed to treat!

The majority of American food tables give the nutritional value of what is said to be a serving or portion. This in practice makes comparisons extremely difficult. These tables are for weights of 100 grammes of the raw materials (or just over 3oz.) You can make your own direct comparisons about the relative values of the selected fruits and vegetables.

THE CHEMICAL COMPOSITION OF THE MAIN RAW JUICE FRUITS AND VEGETABLES

These figures are averages and will vary according to variety, freshness, growing conditions, storage conditions and time of picking. They are a good general guide.
For particulars refer to the descriptions of the individual fruits and vegetables.

Per 100g	Protein (g)	Fat (g)	Carbohydrate (g)	Calories	Na (mg)	K (mg)	Ca (mg)	Mg (mg)	Mn (mg)	Fe (mg)	Cu (mg)	P (mg)	S (mg)	Cl (mg)	Zn (mg)
Alfalfa	18.7						350	4.0	0.035	13	0.08	74	6.0	2.0	0.012
Apple	0.2	tr.	10	35	2.0	100	3.0	12.0	0.01	0.85	0.10	13	5.9	0.7	0.085
Apricot	0.6	tr.	6.5	27	0.5	340	16.0	27.0		0.36	0.12	20.1	16.2	85.6	0.7
Artichoke	3.0	tr.	15	70	2.5	330	50	14	0.18	1.0	0.21	44.0	48.5	36.5	0.76
Asparagus	3.4	tr.	1.0	18	3.3	400	32	30.1	0.08	2.1	0.23	91	18.6	6.0	
Avocado	1.2	8.5	2.5	90	15.0	400	15.3	16	0.08	0.60	0.07	31.0	92	61	0.3
Beetroot	1.3	tr.	6.5	30	85.0	300	25			0.41		32.3			
Brussels sprout	3.5	tr.	4.5	30	9.5	515	29	20	0.11	0.70	0.05	79	103	36	0.37
Cabbage	33.	tr.	3.3	26	6.9	260	45	16	0.06	2.4	0.06	31	89	23	0.14
Carrot	1.0	tr.	4.6	23	85	315	28	9.4	0.01	1.6	0.01	36	7.0	72	0.12
Celery	0.9	tr.	1.3	9	88	245	43	8.6	0.01	1.1	0.005	20	14.9	183	0.065
Comfrey	0.6	tr.													
Cucumber	2.0	tr.	1.8	9	14	150	30	9.0	0.06	0.59	0.08	20.1	12.0	25.6	0.1
Dandelion	2.8	0.5	6.0	45	76.7	400	140	36		3.1		66			
Fennel		0.4	5.1	28		397	100		0.27	2.7	0.08	51			
French beans	0.8	tr.	0.9	28	85	320	25	16		0.4		33		60	0.31
Garlic	6.2	0.2	30.8	137	19	529	29	36		1.5	0.14	202	215	19	
Horseradish	4.5	tr.	11.0	60	8.0	560	120	35.8		2.13		70			
Lemon	0.7	tr.	8	36	1.0	102	22.0	10		0.5		12			
Lettuce	1.0	tr.	1.9	12	3.1	208	26	10	0.07	0.75	0.15	30	12	41	0.25
Onion	1.0	tr.	5.4	26	10	140	22	13	0.08	0.75	0.1	33	52	21	0.11
Orange	0.8	tr.	13	53	3	195	30			0.5	0.07	33	9	4	
Papaya	0.6	tr.	9	39			20			0.5					
Parsley	5.2	tr.	21	21	35	1100	330	56		8.00	0.52	134		160	
Pineapple	0.5	tr.	11.6	46	1.6	247	12	17		0.5	0.08	7.8	2.6	29	
Potato	2.1	tr.	21	88	6.5	570	8	25		0.75	0.15	41	35	79	
Pumpkin	0.6	tr.	3.4	15	1.3	320	40	8		0.4	0.08	20	10.0	37	
Rhubarb	0.6	tr.	1.0	6	2.2	425	103	13.6		0.40	0.13	21	8.2	54	
Spinach	5.4	tr.	1.6	28	363	471	483	84.5		4.5	0.24	95	64	52	
Tomato	0.9	tr.	3.0	16	2.9	300	13.4	11		0.43	0.1	22	11	70	
Turnip	0.8	tr.	3.8	18	58	239	59	7		0.4	0.1	28	22		
Watercress	2.9	tr.	0.7	15	60	314	325	17		1.7	0.2	55	129	160	

THE CHEMICAL COMPOSITION OF THE MAIN RAW JUICE FRUITS AND VEGETABLES – 2

Per 100 g	Carotene (pro Vit A) (mg)	Ascorbic Acid Vitamin C (mg)	Thiamine (mg)	Vit E (mg)	Riboflavin (mg)	Nicotinic Acid (mg)	Pantothenic Acid (mg)	Vitamin B6 (mg)	Biotin (ug)	Folic Acid (ug)
Alfalfa	–	190	0.8	–	1.8	–	3.3	1.0	–	0.8
Apple	0.03	25	0.03	0.7	0.02	0.1	0.07	0.03	0.3	1
Apricot	1.5	8	0.03	–	0.05	0.5	0.3	–	–	3
Artichoke	–	8	0.2	–	0.01	0.1	–	–	–	–
Asparagus	0.5	33	0.18	–	0.20	1.2	0.19	0.06	0.5	100
Avocado	0.1	18	0.07	–	0.15	1.0	–	–	–	20
Beetroot	tr.	6	0.03	–	0.04	0.1	0.12	0.05	tr.	–
Brussels sprout	0.3–2.5	87	0.8	0.1	0.15	0.7	0.4	0.28	0.4	30
Cabbage	6.0–12.0	53	0.05	0.5	0.05	0.25	0.18	0.12	0.1	20
Carrot	6.0–12.0	8	0.06	0.5	0.06	0.6	0.25	0.1	0.6	10
Celery	–	9	0.03	–	0.03	0.3	0.4	0.1	0.1	7
Comfrey	–	100	0.5	–	1.0	5.0	4.2	–	–	–
Cucumber	–	8	0.04	30.0	0.04	0.2	0.3	0.04	–	6
Dandelion	12.5	36	0.12	–	0.15	–	–	–	–	–
Fennel	1.8	31	–	–	–	–	–	–	–	–
French beans	0.5	10	0.05	–	0.1	0.6	0.1	0.1	1.2	–
Garlic	tr.	15	0.25	–	–	0.5	–	–	–	–
Horseradish	–	81	0.07	–	–	–	–	–	–	–
Lemon	–	50	0.05	–	tr.	0.2	0.2	0.06	–	7
Lettuce	1.0–3.0	15	0.07	0.5	0.08	0.3	–	–	–	–
Onion	–	10	0.03	0.3	0.05	0.2	0.1	0.1	0.9	10
Orange	0.05	50	0.08	0.3	0.03	0.2	0.15	0.03	0.8	tr.
Papaya	1.0	100	0.03	–	0.03	0.2	–	–	–	–
Parsley	8	150	0.15	–	0.3	1.0	0.03	0.20	0.4	40
Pineapple	0.06	25	0.08	–	–	0.1	0.17	–	–	4
Potato	tr.	20	0.11	0.1	0.03	1.2	0.3	0.2	0.1	6
Pumpkin	0.9	15	0.05	–	0.04	0.5	–	–	–	–
Rhubarb	0.06	10	0.01	–	0.05	0.2	0.08	0.04	–	3
Spinach	6.0	60	0.12	–	0.20	0.6	0.3	0.1	0.1	80
Tomato	0.7	20	0.06	0.4	0.04	0.6	0.05	0.11	1.2	5
Turnip	6.0	25	0.04	2.3	0.4	0.6	0.02	0.1	0.1	4
Watercress	3	60	0.10	3.1	0.16	0.6	0.1	0.11	0.4	50

KEY All quantities given refer to the amounts present in 100 grams or 3½ ounces. Energy values can also be expressed in joules when 1 calorie is equivalent to 4,184kJ, or 1000 calories to approximately 4,200kJ. The calorie is 1000 calories.
Na = Sodium; K = Potassium; Ca = Calcium; Mg = Magnesium; Mn = Manganese; Fe = Iron; Cu = Copper; P = Phosphorus; S = Sulphur; Cl = Chloride; Zn = Zinc.
tr. indicates a trace as being present.
A dash indicates that reliable information is not available.

FOODS RICH IN IRON

	Iron content mg per 100g
Alfalfa	13.0
Almonds	4.4
Apricots, dried	4.9
Asparagus	2.1
Beetroot leaves	3.2
Cabbage	2.4
Chard	2.5
Cress	2.5
Dandelion leaves	3.2
Flour, 100% wholewheat	3.3
Hazlenuts	4.4
Horseradish	2.1
Kale	2.2
Molasses, crude black	7.9
Oatmeal	4.5
Parsley	8.0
Rice, brown	2.0
Spinach	4.5
Turnip greens	2.4
Yeast, dried brewer's	18.2

About 70% of the iron in our bodies is in the red blood cells as a part of haemoglobin. A deficiency of iron causes anaemia. A further 20% of the iron is stored in the liver, spleen and bone and it is also a component of myoglobin in the muscle cells. Iron is found in serum transferrin and in some enzymes. Iron is essential to the transport of oxygen in the body from the lungs to the cells. It is necessary for the respiration of the cells.

If you are short of either vitamin C or vitamin E, the destruction of the red blood cells becomes considerably faster than is normal so increasing the body's need for iron.

Only about 5-15% of the iron in vegetables is absorbed, so this must be taken into account when taking raw juices for their iron content. An adult man needs at least 10mg per day of iron and a girl or woman who is menstruating needs almost twice as much.

FOODS RICH IN VITAMIN C (ASCORBIC ACID)

	Vit C content mg per 100g
Alfalfa	190
Apple (depending on variety)	25
Blackcurrants	200
Brussels sprouts	87
Cabbage	53
Cauliflower	64
Grapefruit	40
Lemon	50
Orange	50
Papaya	100
Parsley	150
Potatoes, new	30
Potatoes, October-November	20
Potatoes, December	15
Potatoes, January, February	10
Potatoes, March-May	8
Spinach	60
Strawberries	60
Turnip tops	120
Watercress	60

The actions of vitamin C are so numerous as to make it one of the most versatile of vitamins. It is water soluble like the B vitamins and is therefore always in danger of being poured down the sink with the cooking water. With raw juices this is avoided.

The deficiency disease of vitamin C is scurvy which causes bleeding gums, loose teeth, weakness, poor appetite, anaemia, swollen joints, shortness of breath, internal bleeding and eventually death. These things happen because the vitamin is essential for healthy connective tissue, and a shortage causes a breakdown in the collagen.

Most animals can produce their own vitamin C but man cannot either produce it or even store it for very long. Therefore some is needed every day. Each cigarette smoked uses the best part of the usual daily requirement so smokers can choose to give up or to take more C.

There is evidence that Vitamin C protects against arteriosclerosis and heart attacks and as Dr Pauling suggested, is strongly anti-infective in large doses even against the common cold.

The best known natural source of Vitamin C is the acerola or Puerto Rican cherry. Values have been recorded as high as 2,000mg in 100g of fruit. The humble rose hip is also good with an average of about 1,550mg, although there have been reports of samples with 6,000mg.

FOODS RICH IN CALCIUM

	Calcium content mg per 100g
Artichoke	50
Beans, green	50
Beetroot leaves	99
Cabbage	45
Celery	43
Chard	73
Collards	188
Cress	81
Dandelion leaves	140
Horseradish	120
Kale	187
Leeks	52
Parsley	330
Spinach	483
Turnip tops	184
Watercress	222

There is more calcium in the body than any other mineral. An average man will have 2.2 lb, most of which (99%) is in the teeth and bones. Taking enough calcium is not a guarantee that it can be used, for vitamin D is essential to bring about the absorption of calcium. Without that rickets will develop.

Milk is the main provider of calcium and an 8 fl.oz. (225ml) glass will contain 290mg. The dark green vegetables are also good, as can be seen from the table.

The one percent of calcium that is not in the bones is very important for the activity of enzymes in releasing energy for muscular contraction.

Emotional problems and stress reduce the body's ability to absorb calcium, and a pregnant mother must consume enough extra to allow for the building of the baby's bones.

After the age of 55 all people, but especially women, begin to lose calcium from the bones. This condition if it develops excessively is called osteoporosis. The reasons why this happens are not fully understood. Many nutritionists believe that from the age of 55 you should be sure to have sufficient protein, calcium and vitamin D. If osteoporosis is likely then Dr M.R. Urist recommends 1g of calcium, 1000 i.u. vitamin D and 1 to 2g of protein per kg of body weight daily.

CHAPTER 5

JUICERS – HOW TO EXTRACT THE VITAL SUBSTANCES

The ideal juicer will make the maximum amount of liquid from a given quantity of plant material, leaving a quite dry residue behind which, incidentally, makes a first class material for composting organically grown fruits and vegetables.

An electric blender can prepare a juice-like liquid from soft raw materials and is quite good with raspberries and similar fruits although it is usually advisable to add a little water to the mixture before blending. However, for nearly all sources of raw juices the most efficient machine is a purpose built juicing, machine.

These represent a sizeable expenditure for the average family and it is often more economical to buy one where the basic motor unit can perform a number of different functions so that the whole is a useful culinary aid. For example I have a model which is not only a continuous juicer but also shreds or slices for raw salads, blends and chops.

Every type has its own special merits and its particular disadvantages. Which you choose must depend on your individual circumstances, but an experienced health store owner is invariably a good and willing guide. But there are certain points that it is well to be aware of in advance.

Any reasonable manufacturer will give a one year guarantee against faults in manufacture. The machine will be made of high quality plastics and chemically inert metals, such as stainless steel rather than the more reactive aluminium, in places where it is in contact with the juice.

The cheapest type and one that is usually very efficient consists of a basket with perforations into which the fresh materials are put through a feeding hole. There are cutters which divide the matter into fine particles. The basket whirls round expressing the juice through the holes by centrifugal force. After every pint or so of juice has been prepared the machine must be dismantled (always check to see if this is a simple or a tortuous task), the pulp has to be removed, the machine re-assembled and the process repeated. These are excellent value for the moderate user but very tiresome if you want many pints each day.

The next kind is the continuous machine in which the juice comes out of one aperture and the pulp from another. This is very convenient and some makers claim to have juiced two tons of apples without stopping (heaven knows where they put all that juice). In these machines the design of the pulp outlet is very critical for, especially with the softer fruits, there is a risk of clogging which if unnoticed leads to a table covered with leaking liquid and a very messy juicer. Do not be put off for the majority of makers have overcome such faults. Just make certain that you buy on the understood condition that continuous means more or less what it says. The extraction rate is often a little lower than for other types but this is offset by the great convenience.

It is important to remember to clean *all* juicing machines after use or else the rotting and caked-on residue will make a visit to the repairers a premature necessity.

The next class of machine is a hydraulic press which first shreds and then subjects the pulp to between 3,000 and 7,000lb pressure leaving the plant matter almost bone dry. Such a machine is costly and often hard to obtain but probably the most efficient and certainly very desirable for institutional use. It is too large and awkward for normal juicing purposes.

Finally we must consider the non-electric or manual methods of juicing which have, after all, been the only means possible until recently. Very good results are obtainable with a small scale wine press. The fruit or vegetables are chopped and put into a slatted, circular wooden basket. A threaded post runs up the centre and a long lever forces a strong plate downwards onto the material forcing the juice out. A good model will last so well that you may leave it to your heirs.

A good juicer is an investment in health that is small compared to the great benefits you will derive from its regular use. Not only is it essential for therapeutic purposes but, when you are fit and well, fresh raw juices can be prepared into subtle and delicious cocktails of entrancing gastronomic delight. Who else but the hostess with a juicer can offer good health with a drink?

CHAPTER 6

THE JUICES YOU CAN USE

Taking juices may be compared to eating a balanced diet. No one would contemplate trying to live on one single foodstuff. In the same way, most juices tend to work better in combination than alone. The values of one will complement the deficiencies of another.

This chapter goes into the properties of the most important juices. Therapeutic combinations are discussed in the next and, from a study of the values of the single juices, you will be able, when one is unobtainable, to make a substitution that will still be effective.

The very best raw materials should always be used. There is nothing to beat freshly gathered produce from your own organically cultivated garden. But for many crops and for most people, that is not possible. The next best is to buy good looking, fresh fruit and vegetables from the local supplier. Take care to always wash bought produce with clean, flowing water in case there is any contamination.

As soon as a plant is picked, the nutrient value begins to diminish. Canning and bottling both involve cooking which further reduces the vitamin and mineral content some of which also leaks out into the water (that is why you should always try to cook with as little water as possible and to use any left over as a basis for soup, gravy or sauce). Drying foods will of course make them impossible to juice as well as reducing the nutrients.

The only answer is to store high quality materials in a deep freeze. Although there is still a loss, it is not as serious as in other methods of conservation. You may also freeze the actual juice.

How much juice should you take? Some are powerful and are usually taken in combination with the basics such as carrot juice. Less than a pint a day is unlikely to be effective. So the rule to adopt is:

FROM ONE TO EIGHT PINTS OF JUICE A DAY, BUT NEVER MORE THAN IS COMFORTABLE.

It is not always true to say that the more juice the quicker the result, but there is certainly not much benefit to be derived from consuming juice in too small an amount or for a period of less than a month. An experienced practitioner can achieve his results with more or less juices than are recommended here, but he has the benefit of contact with the patient.

WARNING AGAINST SELF-DIAGNOSIS

Here is the point to warn the reader against the self-diagnosis of his complaint, especially if it is serious. No practitioner would diagnose his own complaint without obtaining a second opinion, yet lay people frequently consult no one and prescribe for what they think they have. Many times they can be right but a mistake could be the prelude to an avoidable tragedy.

Raw juice therapy does not conflict with other forms of treatment and is frequently used in conjunction with them. Seek a practitioner sympathetic to natural therapies. This is becoming increasingly less difficult. The President of the giant Merck Sharp and Dohme Research Laboratories, devoted to Pharmaceutical Research said in his Perkins Medal Award Address:

'... in the early 1950's, the pendulum swung from emphasis on natural products to a stress on finding analogues. The result was a unique era in medicinal chemistry, characterized by product profusion and eventually, by public confusion.'

Dr Lewis H. Sarett went on:

'My own view is that, today, the pendulum is swinging back rapidly from analogue research on the time-worn models, and that a renaissance of interest in natural products has begun ...

We are looking more intensely and with better tools at any number of natural regulators, such as the body's mechanisms for maintaining normal blood pressure, assuring muscular tone, repairing gastric damage and controlling moods. We are learning much more about natural defence mechanisms against infections and against neoplasms (cancers). In these and many more areas success depends on broad collaboration within the biomedical community.'

These are words of wisdom from one of the world's leaders of medical research. They give encouragement to natural therapists who have always sought that those with huge financial and human resources should spend more time looking at natural therapies which although perhaps not rapid, are safe, and spend less time seeking drugs marginally more poisonous to the disease than the body but toxic to both.

The plant materials in this chapter are arranged alphabetically and one to the page to facilitate quick and easy reference. The botanical name is included as well as common names to help readers in any difficulty over translation or identification.

ALFALFA
Medicago sativa

This plant, which is also known as lucerne or burn clover, is usually grown to fatten cattle, and the juice has long been employed to put weight on people. Combined with carrot and lettuce juice it is reputed to aid the growth of hair.

Like comfrey the alfalfa has exceptionally long roots, sometimes over 120 feet. These enable the plant to be an efficient concentrator of trace elements. It is a very concentrated source of vitamin A, which is not lost when the plant is dried and sold in tablet form, and of vitamin C, which is.

Not all of us live near a source of alfalfa, but it is as easy to sprout as mustard and cress, and the resulting sprouts are not only of a high nutritional order but are also exceptional providers of a wide spectrum of minerals.

The high vitamin K content is important as a blood clotting factor and has been found in animal studies to control high blood-pressure, although the importance of this to man is not yet established.

The juice is normally taken in combination with carrot because it is very strong alone and the two complement each other well. The protein content is similar to that of raw beef, but it must be said that it is not very tasty so its use as part of a juice combination is the more acceptable way of using alfalfa as part of a healthy diet.

APPLE
Pyrus malus

The Romans knew of more than a score of varieties of apples which must have been selected from the bitter crab apples which are the primitive ancestors of our modern, luscious fruits. England was a cradle of apple development, and many of the most famous types such as Worcester, Cox's Orange Pippin and Laxtons Superb immortalize their grower or locality.

Until the 1930's apples were regarded as an important indicated source of vitamin C. Then some scientist carried out a few analyses which indicated very low amounts of C. It took years for the poor apple to return to favour, for what the chemist found out was partially true. Modern research shows a fluctuation between 2.3mg per 100g, in the worst varieties, to 31.8mg in the best.

Those with high C include Ribston Pippin, Golden Noble, Reinette, Ontario, King of the Pippins, Bramleys, Beauty of Bath, Blenheim Orange, Cox's and Jonathans. The poor providers include Rome Beauty, Laxton's Superb and James Grieve. Around the low middle are such favourites as Golden Delicious and Worcester Pearmain.

Oranges and lemons are more important as providers of vitamin C, but apples, unlike citrus fruits, have very high mineral contents, and also pectins, malic acid and tannic acid, all of which are of the greatest therapeutic importance in normalizing the intestines.

Besides being a great cleanser, apple juice purifies the blood and is helpful for skin and liver, and as a general tonic. After juicing, the liquid often oxidizes quickly so it is best to store for even a short while in the refrigerator.

Apples contain some 10 calories per oz. The vitamins present include C, thiamine, riboflavine, nicotinic acid, carotene, B6, biotin and folic acid. There is a little sodium and a lot of potassium and phosphorus.

Apple juice is good as a drink but vital in overcoming a liverish feeling, in helping sort out digestive disturbances and for flushing the kidneys. Many of these health providing properties are retained in cider vinegar, so if you cannot obtain apples to prepare your juice you can use instead two teaspoonsful of cider vinegar in a glass of water.

APRICOT
Prunus armeniaca

There lives in England a well known vegetarian called Edward Banks who spent many years, and doubtless much effort, in seeking and bringing back to Britain some of those foods from the regions of the Himalyas which have contributed to the legendary fitness of the remote Hunzas. I will never forget the day he gave me some little dried apricots, one of their staple foods, for I recall vividly the delicious flavour and aromatic, heady perfume which made those apricots into the quintessence of all apricots.

Sad to say they are hard to find anywhere dried and, to my knowledge, they are unobtainable in their fresh state so far from their native mountain habitat, for it is certain they would make a superb juice. Fortunately we do have fresh apricots of lesser but still beautiful quality available at many times in the year. The trees have to be picked within about three weeks or else the crop drops to the ground, but different varieties and varying climates extend the season well.

Unlike tomatoes the apricot has about as much vitamin C in its fruit if it is gathered ripe or quite hard. On the other hand the pro vitamin A, carotene, builds up to a high level during the final ripening period so that the fully tree ripened apricot has more than 200% extra.

So, select well coloured, tender fruits that are neither greenish nor tending to shrivel. The perfect fruit will keep for only a day or so before becoming unfit to eat. It is therefore best to freeze the juice, if you can.

In therapy the main use of apricot juice is as an extra provider of vitamin A and in giving a variation to the flavour when incorporated as an addition to other fruit and vegetable juices.

The section on cancer mentions the interest many

doctors have in apricot kernels as being the best way of obtaining nitrilosides. It is worthwhile cracking the stones and adding the kernels to whatever you are juicing. The flavour is not unlike almonds.

ARTICHOKE
Cynara scolymus

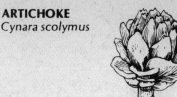

The globe artichoke, or 'choke' as many greengrocers call it, originated in the Mediterranean countries and was a popular delicacy at Roman feasts. It is now grown in many hot areas and is an important crop in parts of California.

A good artichoke will have a nice colour, well closed centre leaves and be without bruises or blemishes. The base should be without any tendency to woodiness. It is often eaten raw as well as cooked, but cooking in an aluminium pot causes discoloration and blackening.

Like other plants in the thistle family, to which it belongs, the artichoke contains some therapeutically valuable oils which have a strong stabilizing effect on the human metabolism. It is used to aid liver complaints and is also a very important diuretic for those suffering from the retention of water.

Most writers on juices have ignored these virtues which have nevertheless been known in Italy, France and Germany for many centuries. In those lands the artichoke forms the basis for several drinks which are fortified with alcohol. You can try one yourself with diuretic powers by juicing 2oz. (50g) of the leaves and adding both juice and the residual pulp to a bottle of white wine. Leave for a week, strain into a clean bottle and it is ready for use. A wineglassful each day is the normal amount to take.

This is a useful recipe because artichokes are not always available and there are great price fluctuations. With wine you can take the juice whenever you wish. This is called 'artichoke elixir' in the therapeutic index.

The juice is not normally taken alone, but is mixed with others and, where its use is suggested, it can be fresh, frozen or with wine. It is not a very good source of Vitamin C, but is very rich in calcium.

ASPARAGUS
Asparagus officinalis

Asparagus is a luxury vegetable that sill grows wild in mediterranean countries. Old herbals called it sparrowgrass and farmers still call the plant 'grass'. A big helping will contain less than 40 calories and it is a good provider of vitamin C, folic acid and potassium.

The therapeutically active substance found in the asparagus is the alkaloid asparagine which exerts a rapid effect upon the kidneys, stimulating them and colouring the urine a dark yellow within hours of consumption. The asparagine is much reduced in quantity during cooking, so that the use of quite a small amount of the raw juice produces a good diuretic effect.

Not only is the urine coloured, the asparagus also imparts quite a strong smell to it, so do not think anything is amiss should this phenomenon surprise you. The essential oils which give asparagus its distinctive and pleasant flavour are very powerful because they are present in such small amounts that special analytical methods have to be employed to detect them.

Asparagus juice is usually taken in the quantity of a sherry-glassful three times a day before meals. It has been used not only to remove water from the body but as a purifier of the blood, to tone up the nervous system and as a gentle laxative.

The thickness of the asparagus used has little effect upon the value, only upon the cost. So choose fresh looking stems that have not dried out and gone floppy. The white, woody base of the stem helps prevent it from losing moisture. It can be stored for a few days wrapped with a damp cloth around the base and kept in a cool place.

AVOCADO
Persea gratissima or
Persea americana

This is known sometimes as the alligator pear because of the texture of its skin and its pear-like shape. The usual name is derived from a Central American name of the greatest antiquity, ahuacatl. They were first appreciated by the Spanish conquistadores who noted that the Incas cultivated the fruit.

The avocado contains a good supply of carotene, pro vitamin A, there being three times as much in a well-coloured ripe fruit as in a hard one. Analysts have found no less than 11 vitamins and 17 minerals in the fruit, making it a very comprehensive storehouse of the nutritional needs of man. There is a high level of oil which contains the vitamins A, D and E, and, although the calorie count is large, there being 165 calories in 100g, it is of nutritional worth.

There is evidence quoted, but not in detail, by Dr Magnus Pyke in *Food and Society* suggesting that the leaves and fruits of the avocado have been shown to contain a substance known to be somewhat toxic to goats, rabbits, horses and canaries. There is no evidence that there is any danger to man, but for the sake of prudence it is best to have no more than one avocado a day whether juiced or fresh.

Happily the fate of the unfortunate canary need not affect the use of avocado juice in the therapy because the best effect is found when the juice is employed as an external application to the skin.

The juice is a good way of having a balanced quantity of the oil of avocado. This oil is second only to lanolin in being the most penetrating oil known when applied to the human skin. Yet, unlike lanolin which is thought by many experts to be the cause of more cases of sensitivity to cosmetics than any other ingredient, avocado is emollient and innocuous without any known sensitizing effects.

It can therefore be used externally as the ideal treatment for soothing sensitive skins. Avocado reduces ultra violet light and is a useful sunscreening lotion for use prior to moderate exposure to the sun's rays.

BEETROOT
Beta vulgaris

The old Greeks looked upon the beet as being good for cooling the blood. The Romans followed this up and used the juice as a specific against feverish conditions, especially in growing children. Later generations found that there was also a very strong specific action for regulating the digestive system.

The *Doctrine of Signatures*, which suggests that every plant illustrates its medical purpose, supposed that beet, because of its redness, was good for the blood. In fact the iron content is not particularly high, although it is said to be present in a form that is easy to assimilate.

The whole beet family (remember sugar beet) is rich in easily digested carbohydrates, even so the calorie content is not high, although it increases when boiled. The red beetroot tends to concentrate rather than lose its mineral content when boiled for two hours, but the vitamins are generally reduced. Therefore when used therapeutically beetroot is usually juiced raw.

The protein factors or amino acids are good both in quality and quantity. The minerals found abundantly include the salts of phosphorus, sodium, calcium, potassium and magnesium. The taste has a stimulating effect not only upon the nerves of the tongue but also on the nerves in the intestines.

In France there have been many experiments on the use of very large quantities of beet juice, six or seven pints a day, to aid recovery in case of malignant disease. Some promising results have been reported but there is far too little evidence yet to draw even tentative conclusions. In Germany there is widespread use of beet juice, which is available in pasteurized form in bottles, as a powerful restorative during convalescence.

It follows that beets are also good for general weakness and debility of all sorts. In combination with other juices, especially carrot and cucumber, the beet juice is not only a splendid blood builder but also one of the finest therapies for sexual weakness, kidney stones, gall bladder, kidney, liver and prostate troubles.

Beet juice still remains a potent force the secrets of which are far from being unlocked. It is, after carrot, one of the chief juices in the science of natural healing as practised on the Continent. The choline present acts to regulate digestion by controlling the peristalsis, or natural rhythmical contractions of the gut and, because of this, the assimilation of food during the time of recovery is much assisted.

Uncooked beets keep rather better than many vegetables. If you do cook them it is important to avoid damaging or cutting the skin. If this happens the red colour will leach out into the cooking water leaving the cook with a very pale beet of unattractive appearance. If the skin is accidently damaged the leakage of colour will be very much reduced if you add a few drops of lemon juice or cider vinegar to the water.

The dark green beet tops should not be discarded because they are rich in vitamin A and in minerals. They may be juiced in small quantities as an addition to other juices, whilst steamed they make a good and cheap alternative to spinach.

BRUSSELS SPROUT
*Brassica oleracea
var. gemmifera*

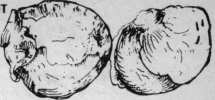

You will see from the botanical name that the brussels sprout is a variety of the cabbage family. The early Dutch gardeners were not only skilled at creating new varieties of tulip; they also produced a number of new vegetables by selectively breeding with wild cabbage (*Brassica maritime*).

They are very important nutritionally because they have a long season and are one of the top providers of vitamin C, a cupful weighting 100g will give, when raw, 100mg of vitamin C, which is twice as much as the same weight of orange. After boiling the C goes down to 35mg – a good example of the benefit of using the whole raw juice to obtain the best nutritive value. If you do want to cook the sprouts as a vegetable it is wise to remember that it is best to steam them until just tender in as little water as possible, which should be fast boiling before the sprouts go in. Any remaining water can always be used for soup or in gravy. Why throw vitamins and minerals down the sink?

Brussels sprout juice is often used with runner or string bean juice as a treatment for diabetes in adults. Children who have diabetes often do not have the ability to produce insulin, but in adults it can happen that there is a defect not in the production but in the supply. Diabetes can be a serious condition unless it is expertly managed by a qualified practitioner who will advise on individual treatment, but the brussels sprout and runner bean mixture has been reported to be a valuable aid to treatment.

CABBAGE
Brassica oleracea
var. capit. alb.

The white cabbage has been the subject of a wide variety of very interesting medical papers, but no research centre has followed up the remarkable preliminary work. It appears possible that the usual lack of finance for natural cures is the reason. Only drugs bring the profits needed for full scale trials.

It is likely, say archaeologists, that the cabbage was one of the first vegetables to be cultivated. This is important nutritionally because it could well be the case that man has built up a relationship with the cabbage's complex and valuable nutritional content.

Dr O'Dell and his co-workers, in submitting a paper at the fifth International Congress of Nutrition in Washington, reported that the addition of cabbage to a completely balanced feed for female guinea pigs produced a very much increased growth and a much improved resistance to infection from the virulent mouse-typhus. Dr Rudat, whilst confirming the work of O'Dell, found similar results with garlic when experimenting with the anti-biotic properties of certain plants.

This activity is thought likely to be as a result of the essential oils that occur naturally in plants. Professor Schuphan has commented that, both in manufactured foods and even in the home, we are usually omitting (or replacing with a synthetic) those pot-herbs and spices which, it seems likely, nowadays have a valuable nutritive and protective function for man.

It is precisely because of our changing life style that juice therapy has today a part to play in restoring to man those nutrients and trace elements that are so commonly lacking in modern food. The compelling evidence in this book may not convince the professional sceptic but will surely lead the open minded towards a better understanding of the way our bodies have become used to and dependent upon nutritional factors which they no longer have in sufficient quantity.

The unknown dietary factors in cabbage are obviously impossible to identify, but the factor that is said to have an astonishingly good record of success against gastric ulcers has been called vitamin U.

This factor does not seem to be diminished in effectiveness when the cabbage is concentrated, and successes are common with both the raw juice and with other forms. Dr Cheney found in a test with a hundred ulcer victims that the pain went in an average of five days and that healing had occured by the fourteenth day except in very serious cases. The usual time expected for such a result is about seven weeks.

Dr Hannon wrote to the *American Medical Association Journal* with news of the good results obtained in patients with digestive conditions of long-standing, that had proved resistant to normal treatment, by giving raw cabbage juice. He claimed that they were cured in spite of being sceptical of this last resort approach.

Cabbage and cabbage juice should never be taken so that they become the main part of the diet. Very excessive intakes have been known to cause the thyroid disease called goitre. It is in normal amounts that cabbage comes valuable nutritionally and that the juice, which is bitter and not delicious, assumes its role as a necessary part of the natural treatment of infections, ulcers and other disorders of the digestive system.

In the treatment of ulcers Dr Cheney, in whose trial only five out of a hundred patients failed to show improvement, gave 16 fl.oz. (450ml) of the raw juice each day, in small regular doses.

CARROT
Daucus carota

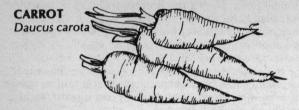

The carrot provides what is certainly the most important basic juice. The yellow colour is due to a substance called carotene. Another name for carotene is *pro vitamin A*. Many authors write that carrots contain a lot of vitamin A, this is not actually true, what the carrot does contain is the pro vitamin. That means a substance that is converted by the body into the vitamin itself.

Dr W. Kübler states that the carrot plays the most important part in an infants supply of vitamin A. He goes on to point out that when carrots are fed jointly with milk, the utilization of carotene as vitamin A is considerably increased. He recommends that a carrot milk juice is the ideal vitamin A source for infants and can in no case lead to the risk of the child having too much A.

On the other hand Professor Werner Schuphan, who is director of the German Insitute of Plant Products, has conducted many hundreds of analyses of different varieties of carrot and found that while many contain a lot of carotene, some have only a little.

This is important because carrots are widely used. Indeed it is estimated that in Germany carrots account for 10% of the total vegetable consumption. From the juice point of view, the varieties to be employed are ideally those with the most carotene. It is fortunate that the pro vitamin is strongly coloured for this means that so long as you use good coloured carrots they are likely to be the best nutritionally speaking too.

As a general rule, early carrots are pale and low in carotene. Two exceptions, according to Professor Schuphan, are Geisenheim forcing and Amsterdam forcing, these form carotene early and are also tender. Because carotene is not water soluble, but is fat soluble, there is not a very great deterioration in the vitamin content on storage.

The other important minerals and vitamins present in carrots do not vary very much from variety to variety. Besides the carotene, there are significant amounts of the vitamins thiamine, riboflavine, nicotinic acid, ascorbic acid (vitamin C), pantothenic acid, B6, biotin, folic acid and the minerals potassium, sodium, calcium, magnesium, iron, phosphorus, sulphur, copper and chlorine.

Nursing mothers are well advised, for the sake of the quality of their milk, to take carrot juice throughout lactation. When the baby is on the way it is also important to not only drink the juice but also good sense to nibble a carrot when you feel hungry. For although a good sized one will provide your minimum requirement of vitamin A, 7oz. (200g) of carrot contain only 45 calories and will help keep you slim.

The carrot is recorded as being used in medicine by the early Greeks and has been cherished ever since. Its juice is one of the most delicious and healthful, and alone or in combination should be in every daily diet providing, as it does, the essential vitamin A, without the saturated fats with which this vitamin is associated in eggs and butter.

CELERY
Apium graveolens

The medical virtues of celery were first described by the Greeks Discorides and Pliny. In the early middle ages celery was in common use for stones, constipation, menstrual problems and for disorders of the liver and gall bladder.

The green leaves and stem and the bulbous root are all extremely rich in active ingredients that make celery a very important medicinal plant. There is a well balanced content of the basic minerals, vitamins and nutrients, but in addition there are important concentrations of plant hormones and the essential oils that give celery its strong and characteristic smell. These oils have a specific effect on the regulation of the nervous system, and have a great calming influence.

Celery is used for its strong stimulating effect on a weak sexual system, but as is usual with plant therapies the normally active person does not have to fear an uncontrollable upsurge. Plant therapy tends to make the system normal. Like beet there is also a general tonic effect.

The strong diuretic (water removing) powers of celery enable it to be used as a help in the control of arthritis and rheumatism. Sufferers cannot have too much and may consume the vegetable cooked or raw, or in juice form which is the most effective treatment of all.

A tablespoonful of honey in celery juice, sipped slowly, will very effectively reduce the appetite if taken before a meal, and makes a delightful drink. You can take the same mixture as a nightcap when it will help you to relax into a soothing and restful sleep.

Those who take the juice who have in the past suffered from a tendency towards stones in the gall bladder or the kidneys usually find that these painful deposits cannot form again. It seems likely that this effect is related to the anti-arthritic properties of the juice.

Celery is a good source of chlorides, potassium and sodium but in other respects the vitamin and minerals are simply adequate rather than remarkable. It is the presence of the essential oils which makes celery special. These are also found in the seeds and, if available, they too can be added to the juice.

COMFREY
Symphytum
caucasicum
et peregrinum

Comfrey has been recorded as a medicine since the ancient Greeks and Romans used an ointment from it to heal wounds and a medicine to cure ulcers. There are various ideas as to where the modern name originated, perhaps from the Latin *confervere* meaning to knit together. The botanical name comes from the Greek *sumphuo*, to unite. there has never been any doubt about the healing powers.

The active principle is allantoin which, according to the *Extra Pharmacopoeia* of Martindale is said to be a cell proliferant and healing agent stimulating healthy tissue formation; it has been used in the treatment of gastric ulcer, and it is an ingredient of some skin preparations.

Modern research has shown a great and unexpected nutritional benefit. Comfrey is one of the very few plants which contain vitamin B_{12}. This vitamin prevents pernicious anaemia, and vegetarians are at some risk from being deficient if they do not take any dairy products. The body stores enough for five or six years, so the strict vegan may appear to be well for a long time before any deficiency begins to show.

The Russian comfrey, which is used as a crop and as a fine source of compost as well as being nutritionally good, stands three feet high, the wild comfrey, *Symphytum officinale*, is lower, but can be used instead. There is a famous Bavarian recipe which uses the leaves on stalks, dipped in an egg and flour batter and deep fried; or the plant can be cooked like spinach.

As a juice it is used for its valuable vitamin content and in cases of ulcers, fractures and wounds. In healing the protein content must be very important, because the healing process uses such protein at a time when the patient does not feel like eating. The fresh plant has 3-4% protein and the dried 21-22%. Young roots may be added to leaves when juicing.

Comfrey takes many years to grow from seed, but can be easily propagated from root cuttings.

CUCUMBER
Cucumis sativus

When the cucumber became important as a food in the eighteenth century, it did not take long for people to forget those medical properties which had been well-known first of all to the Greeks and Romans and then later on to the Arab physicians.

Today we see the cucumber as a provider of a juice renowned for its properties as an increaser of the flow of urine and as a complement to the effects of celery and carrot juice for rheumatic conditions, while at the same time being a glamorous skin lotion.

Japanese research in the first half of this century indicated that there was a valuable substance present in the juice for the treatment of the whole intestinal tract. Sad to say this work has not been pursued and the active factor still retains the secret of its identity.

Cucumber is very low in calories, about 3 per ounce being an average figure. Very high potassium contents have been claimed for the plant which from the most up-to-date analyses available would seem to be an exaggeration. It is simply a good provider, almost identical in fact to the beetroot. The vitamin content is also generally to be found between low and average for the edible vegetable.

Nevertheless cucumber juice is certainly a valuable part of the treatment of rheumatic conditions. It does not matter too much that the reason for this effect is not clear. What is important is that it helps many sufferers.

Although the whole juice is the best skin lotion it is worth remembering that the peel itself, like lemon peel, should always be retained and used on the hands especially after they have been in a strong detergent or in very hot water. It is not necessary to rub hard – indeed skin care with cucumber should be a gentle, fragrant art.

DANDELION
Taraxacum officinale

The humble dandelion is so often seen as an annoying weed in the garden and in the farmer's fields. Yet this attractive golden sunburst is a herbal medicine of renowned effect and great antiquity. The Germans call it Löwenzahn, or Lions tooth, but the French Pissenlit, which means 'wet the bed' is more descriptive of its diuretic properties.

In Belgium the plant is grown as a crop. The leaves when young are a tasty salad vegetable and the roots can be dried, roasted and then ground as a good coffee substitute without caffeine and which has beneficial effects on indigestion and on rheumatic complaints.

Nutritionally the dandelion is remarkable value containing almost as much iron as spinach, quadruple the vitamin A content of lettuce plus very rich supplies of magnesium (some think dandelion the best source of all), potassium, vitamin C, calcium and sodium.

The botanical name *Taraxacum* comes from a Greek word which means to alter or to stir up and this refers to its medical properties. The specific word *officinale* used to be given to all officially recognized herbs.

The secret of growing your own is to use well dug soil and then to remove the flowers as soon as they appear. This avoids the random seeding of the plant and ensures a lush growth of leaves for several years. It is best to select seeds from a broad leafed variety as those are more tender and juicy.

The readily available organic magnesium makes the juice of the leaves with or without the roots very valuable for all bone disorders. It is often mixed with the juices of the leaves of carrots and turnips.

With the juices of the stinging nettle and watercress it is the ideal basis for a 'spring clean' and is used this way in Germany as part of a two week course combined with a diet without meat or much sugar or starch. This treatment helps to make the liver and the gall bladder normal, and it has a beneficial effect upon the nervous system.

As a diuretic, it can be taken alone. The Romans called the plant *Herba urinaria*, but this effect is the consequence of a dose of several ounces a day, whereas for other uses 2 fl.oz. (50ml) is sufficient.

FENNEL
Foeniculum vulgare

The fennel, or finocchio as the Italians call it, is a versatile vegetable which can not only be eaten cooked or raw but is also a basis for anise, and is one of the ingredients of licorice. It flavours some brandy-based drinks, whilst the leaves are an important culinary herb.

It is not surprising then that the plant and its juice contain some valuable constituents. The nutrients are similar to those in celery, which belongs to the same family, but it is the essential oil that is the basis for its good action on an upset stomach and its stimulating properties. The oil is present in relatively large amounts, from 3-6% of the total weight.

The Greeks called fennel *marathron* which derived from their word meaning to become slim, later the Emperor Charlemagne ensured that it was grown on all his farms. He, and other people in early times, thought fennel gave courage and was good for the eyes. Bedrooms were protected from the evil spirits of the night with fennel in the keyholes. The plant was an essential component of the wreath used above the door on midsummer day to keep the witches quiet.

Insects keep away from fennel so the floors were spread with stalks so that the fleas kept their distance. The stalks were cooked as an alternative to asparagus, or put under bread while it was baking to give it an aromatic flavour.

With carrot juice, fennel is very good for night blindness or optic weakness. These two plus beet juice make a good remedy for anaemia especially the sort resulting from excessive menstruation.

Fennel juice forms part of formulae for convalescence and for indigestion. The French use it for migraine and dizziness where good results have been noted. The vitamin C content is said to be very high and there are also, in addition to the oil, vitamins A and B complex, calcium, sulphur, iron, phosphorus and potassium.

FRENCH OR STRING BEAN
Phaseolus vulgaris

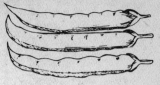

These are the beans known in France as *haricot verte* and if they are allowed to become old, they become the dried haricot beans. Like all green beans, if they are sliced before cooking the loss of flavour and nutrients into the water is considerable. The fresh juice is not very high in any particular vitamin or mineral constituent but is well balanced.

Therapeutically it is used as a nervous stimulant and a number of practitioners have said that the juice stimulates the production of insulin. It is usually used for this purpose in combination with brussels sprout juice. Treatment for diabetes should, however, always be under the control of a practitioner.

French bean juice is recommended during convalescence and for gout. The usual dose is quite small, about half a glass or 5 fl.oz. (150ml) a day being sufficient for these purposes.

The diabetic, who must in any case be on a strictly controlled diet, needs rather more. The usual requirement is 10 fl.oz. (275ml) a day with an equal amount of brussels sprout juice.

GARLIC
Allium sativum

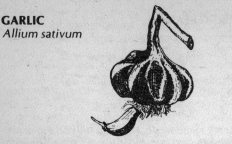

Nicholas Culpeper begins his description of garlic with these words: 'The offensiveness of the breath of him that hath eaten Garlick, will lead you by the nose to the knowledge hereof, and (instead of a description) direct you to the place where it groweth in gardens, which kinds are the best and most physical.'

He goes on to say how it used to be called the poor man's treacle because it was his remedy for all diseases and hurts. The old Greeks placed garlic on stones at cross roads as a dinner for their triple godess Hecate who was Diana on earth, Phoebe in heaven and Prosperine in hell.

Like the onion, garlic has a powerful effect on healing wounds but is also very good as a disinfectant and as such many tons were used to treat wounds during the hell of the first world war. When the plague ravaged Marseilles in 1722 four robbers claimed that a mixture, later called Four Thieves Vinegar, and in which an important ingredient was garlic, protected them from the plague as they stole from dead victims.

As with horseradish, it is difficult to juice garlic in the machine because of the strong essential oils which can only be removed with the greatest difficulty. So we crush it and the resulting liquid is easily incorporated into juices or taken in small amounts by itself.

In 1936 Caspari demonstrated in the laboratory that garlic can destroy the staphylococcus and that this might be the basis for the use of garlic as a medicine. Later on studies with animals demonstrated the effect of garlic in improving the condition of arteriosclerosis whilst at the same time bringing down the blood-pressure.

Garlic acts well against catarrh, particularly in smokers, and for colds. Like onion juice, one dessertspoonful of garlic in half a pint of warm water is a recognized remedy for worms in children. One suspects that Italian children must be well protected against worms, and statistics show that they have a lower incidence of heart disease than most Europeans, all of which helps to confirm the therapeutic value of this bulb.

Work by Dr Weiss of Chicago elegantly demonstrates the great benefit received in a controlled trial on sufferers from long-standing intestinal disorders such as persistent diarrhoea with accompanying headaches. These symptoms went in the patients having garlic, but even more importantly, an entirely fresh and improved quality was found in the intestinal flora, those bacteria which aid the digestion of food.

Garlic has been used successfully for many conditions including those mentioned already plus tuberculosis, enterocolitis and amoebic dysentry. It is an expectorant as well as assisting asthma and bronchitis.

This food has been used as a medicine for some 5,000 years and we would be misguided not to use it on account of the smell. If you cannot bear to use it with your juices then take garlic in the form of capsules which do not dissolve until they have reached the intestine.

HORSERADISH
Cochlearia armoracia

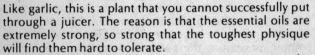

Like garlic, this is a plant that you cannot successfully put through a juicer. The reason is that the essential oils are extremely strong, so strong that the toughest physique will find them hard to tolerate.

Horseradish is therefore made up as a sauce by shredding and pounding the fresh root to which is added lemon juice. In this form it can be stored in a cold place for at least a week.

This herb is a wonderful solvent for mucus in the nose and sinus. Take a half teaspoonful of the sauce without dilution both morning and afternoon. Do not drink anything or eat for at least ten minutes after the dose, there will be a powerful feeling in the head, sometimes with sweating and usually accompanied by many tears (not of pain).

Sinus troubles cause much pain and misery. The horseradish attacks the very cause of the condition and brings relief. Sometimes it is necessary to continue the treatment for several months, but you will know when the horseradish has done its work because the violent sensations resulting from the use of the sauce will gently reduce and finally almost disappear along with the mucus.

It is a good idea to combine this treatment with the juices of radish, including both leaves and root, and carrot. These two will help to rebuild the tissues ravaged by the sinus infection. You will understand that it is also vital to make sure that your eating pattern becomes well-balanced with the avoidance of refined carbohydrates and the adoption of a basically natural diet.

Horseradish is also specific for water retention, or dropsy, as it used to be called. This is tied in with a stimulating effect on the blood capillaries caused by the action of the main therapeutic principal in the plant, a glycoside called sinigrin. Horseradish has a surprisingly high vitamin C content, almost 40mg to 1oz. (25g) – this is one of the highest vegetable concentrations, eight times that of lettuce and two thirds that of blackcurrants. It has as well one of the highest amounts of potassium and sulphur, with unusually rich stores of manganese and calcium.

Other uses that have been identified are for diabetics, where Professor Kuhn found an improvement in the blood picture, for coughs and catarrh and in the treatment of circulatory problems of a mild nature.

LEMON
Citrus limonia

Lemonade is known to have been used as a refreshing drink since the time of the Moguls. Modern investigations have tended to support this use, the essential oil being very good for cooling the body. This use can be extended to the employment of lemon juice with water and sugar as the best drink to take when you have a fever.

When the temperature of the body is high, whether from the effects of the sun or from the results of illness, it is necessary to take regular drinks in order to prevent dehydration. Sugar is not normally a desirable part of a healthy diet, nevertheless it has its part to play with lemon, although there is no doubt that the addition of honey if available is very much to be preferred.

The high vitamin C content of the lemon has been used for hundreds of years to ward off scurvy among sailors and travellers. There is also much calcium but little sodium, so the fruit is good as a flavouring for those on a low salt diet.

Because in some countries the producers of lemons extend their keeping properties and improve appearance by coating them with the chemical, diphenyl and waxing the fruits, it is a wise precaution to wash the lemon with a little unscented soap and then rinse thoroughly before converting the whole fruit to juice.

The pulp left from the juicing is excellent for the skin and can also soothe the bites and stings of insects. If you add equal parts of toilet water and of glycerine to the residue the mixture can be made to keep the hands smooth.

Doctors Morel and Rochaix demonstrated that the extract of lemon when vapourized will neutralize the bacteria of meningococcus, typhoid, pneumocoocus and staphylococcus in from between 15 and 180 minutes.

A gastronomically inclined Frenchman, Charles Richet, is said by Dr Valnet to have discovered that the lemon juice added to raw oysters before eating them destroys 92% of the bacteria present within 15 minutes. A good reason to wait before you eat! There must also remain a doubt about the remaining 8% and their potential toxicity.

This information is relevent to the idea that lemon juice is a most important therapy to be used in all cases of infection of the respiratory tract and as a general tonic.

Provided that the juice is diluted with water, there is no danger in taking any reasonable quantity of lemon juice. Be sure to choose firm, clear coloured lemons that have not begun to wither. The first signs of aging can be spotted where the stem was once attached to the fruit.

LETTUCE
Lactuca sativa
or *Lactuca virosa*

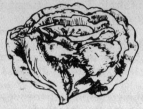

Lettuce is one of the most delicate salad plants – there is usually nothing but disappointment to be gained from trying to bring a wilting specimen back to life. It has been cultivated since the earliest times, and varieties such as Cos or Romaine had become popular by the middle ages.

Culpeper, the old English herbalist said, 'The juice of lettuce mixed with oil of roses, applied to the forehead and temples procureth sleep and easeth the head-ache.' He goes on to say that when taken 'it abateth bodily lust.' This, it seems, is an accurate observation. Lettuce juice has been likened in effect to the sedative action of opium without the accompanying excitement.

H.M. Evans of the University of California demonstrated in a series of experiments that whilst the lettuce had a calming effect on sexual ardour, there was a surprisingly strong compensatory effect in that the rate of fertility was greatly increased. So although the normal person might well find these two results to be incompatible (or at any rate inconceivable) lettuce is frequently suggested to help men who suffer from premature ejaculation.

Pythagoras, the ancient Greek mathematician, therefore knew only half of this information when he called lettuce 'The plant of the eunuchs'. This compensation results from a mixture of tonic and sedative components in which the calming effect on the nervous system and digestive organs as well as the sexual is combined with a tonic action upon the glands.

There is a slight laxative action with the unusual feature that the odour of ill-smelling stools is often much improved. The mineral content is rich so that lettuce is a good restorer of mineral balance. Among those present are iodine, phosphorus, iron, copper, calcium, cobalt, zinc, manganese and potassium.

The vitamin content includes a good deal of pro vitamin A, but it is essential to bear in mind that the outer leaves may contain fifty times more than the white inside leaves, so juice everything. Vitamins B, C and E are also present.

The strong therapeutic effect results from the many alkaloids present. These include asparagine (see *asparagus*), lactucine, lactucic acid and hyoscyamine.

A mixture of lettuce and spinach juice is said to help the growth of hair if drunk to the extent of a pint or so a day. So much hair loss is caused by your genetic inheritance and not through deficiencies that this information is given for the sake of the desperate.

There is much more evidence for its effectiveness in dealing with a nervous cough and as supportive therapy which might help but not cure the diabetic and the asthmatic and help ease those who have continuous pain.

NETTLE
Urtica dioica
et urens

The stinging nettle (which is called *ortie* in France and *Brennessel* in Germany) was said to be introduced into Britain by Caesar's soldiers. They sowed it along the sides of the great straight roads, both the roads and the nettles survive. At the end of a day's match the cooler climate of England and the weary miles made their legs ache. They would gather the nettles and beat each other with them so warming the affected parts. Really an embrocation for the strong.

Culpeper says wittily that they may be found by feeling on the darkest night! He tells us that the juice with honey is a safe and sure medicine to open the pipes and passages of the lungs.

Today the herbal practitioner has found many uses for the humble nettle. The extract with alcohol is a stimulating hair tonic. Urtication, or beating with nettles is sometimes used as a counter irritant for rheumatic sufferers. It is given to lessen bleeding in the mouth, in the form of a juice, and the juice will apparently greatly relieve painful piles or haemorrhoids if taken a table-spoonful at a time, three times a day.

The active constituents are many and include 5-hydroxytryptamine, histamine, formic acid and gallic acid, plus much readily assimilable iron. Research by Drs Herrmann and Neumann established that an increased metabolic rate some 75% higher than usual took place over a period which lasted from the sixth to the twenty-second hour after taking a glassful. They said that this was very helpful when used in conjunction with therapies for removing toxins from the blood, and for rheumatism.

For the same reason, nettle juice is a good addition to any iron therapy for anaemia. It helps control diarrhoea and is at the same time a diuretic which aids the elimination of uric acid. It is powerful so is usually taken a wineglassful at a time. The part of the plant to pick is the top leaves, you may wear gloves or 'Grasp it like a man of mettle and it soft as silk remains.'

Research by Dr Keeser found that the nettle could reduce the blood sugar level. The juice is often good for nervous eczema.

The White Dead Nettle (*Lamium album*) although similar in appearance, belongs to a completely different botanical family, but it acts as an astringent and is also effective for diarrhoea.

ONION
Allium cepa

Onions possess many of the properties of garlic without being so socially devastating, but there are particular benefits that are to be found in garlic alone and uses for which the onion is far better suited than its partner.

The ancient Egyptians drew pictures of the onion in their funeral chambers in a way which signified that it had for them a holy status. The Greeks and Romans used the juice for all digestive problems, later it was esteemed as a purifier of the blood. The Germans used it for nerve pains such as occur in the stumps of amputated limbs.

The essential oils which give the onion its pungency are also responsible for its therapeutic effects which include a normalizing effect on the sympathetic nervous system and a stimulating effect upon the growth of the most beneficial of the bacteria which carry out their activities in our guts.

More than 200 years ago doctors were using a mixture of milk and onion juice to remove worms from children, and there is a well-known practitioner in Germany today whose work has shown that his predecessors were right. Professor Heubner believes it to be not only effective but, unlike many vermifuges, safe.

Today, onion juice is mostly used for catarrh, especially that persistent sort which sometimes follows colds but which is not serious enough to require the dynamite-like effect of the horseradish cream. It should also be taken as a routine measure during the treatment of diseases of the respiratory tract including coughs, colds, bronchitis and hoarseness. Infants and growing children often find the onion juice is more palatable when mixed with warm water and honey.

Nicholas Culpeper, the great herbalist, said that the

onion was owned by the planet Mars and it had the power to draw corruption to it. For this reason it was a common ingredient of poultices. With vinegar, he says that onion juice removes blemishes from the skin and, two hundred years before the German report, prescribed it for worms in children.

Nutritionally the onion is fairly average containing useful but not very large quantities of the usual vitamins and minerals, with more sugars than many vegetables which contribute to the 7 calories to be found in an ounce.

ORANGE
Citrus sinensis

The botanical name given is for the common or Malta orange which was introduced into Europe from China and is now grown in many hot countries especially the U.S.A. Among other species are the *Citrus aurantium* which is the bitterly aromatic Seville orange and the *Citrus sinensis* or sweet orange. The most scented species is the *Citrus bergamia* from which the orange bergamot is prepared.

The first greenhouses were called 'orangeries' because the fruit is damaged by even a slight frost, and the nobles of seventeenth-century England and France would not allow so unpredictable a thing as the weather to stand between them and their enjoyment of this delicious fruit.

The orange has a modest mineral content but a good ripe fruit will have from 50-100 mg of vitamin C in 100g, a smallish fruit. There are also plenty of the interesting and probably important bioflavonoids, or vitamin P. There is much experience which strongly suggests that when vitamin C is taken, for example as an anti-infective, the effect is reinforced in the presence of these bioflavonoids.

In nature they are often found naturally occuring in vitamin C-rich fruits such as rose hips and green peppers. Other names for the bioflavonoids include rutin and hesperidin. They have been used in concentrated form for the treatment of high blood-pressure, as anti-coagulants and as part of the treatment for colds.

Orange juice is very nutritious and pleasant to take at any time, but it is a good idea to take a regular glass daily during the winter months to make certain that you are having enough vitamin C. The fat soluble vitamins, A, D and E can be stored in the body, but you need your vitamin C regularly.

PAPAYA
Carica papaya

The papaya is an amazingly rich source of the proteolytic enzymes. These are the chemicals that make the digestion of protein possible when you eat. Papain, which is the most important of these enzymes in the papaya, is extracted and dried as a powder for use to aid the digestion, and it is often used as a meat tenderizer, the enzyme partially breaking down the meat fibres – digesting them in fact.

Many experts, such as Dr Lytton-Bernard, have claimed rejuvenating properties for papaya, especially for the control of premature ageing. It may be that it works simply because a poor digestion leaves the body without the correct nutrients. Those who find it almost impossible to digest anything frequently find that papaya used regularly, either in tablet or juice form, marks the turning point in the climb back to vitality and good health.

As a cleanser you can take a quarter pint of papaya juice alternated each hour for twelve hours by the same amount of cucumber or green bean juice. Papaya loses some of the enzymes as it ripens, so if you have the choice select them green. They are easy to obtain in most parts of America but are not found in British greengrocers very often. Fortunately there has been a rapid expansion in the numbers of specialist shops providing for the needs of the Indian and West Indian communites where papayas can be bought.

Papaya contains arginine which is known to be essential for male fertility and also carpain, an enzyme thought to be good for the heart. Fibrin also occurs and this substance is not commonly found in the plant kingdom, in man it forms part of the blood clotting process. The papaya has very little fat but has 0·6% protein and very high levels of vitamins A and C.

Because of the enzymes it has been recommended for use as a part of the treatment for cancer and this is discussed in more detail in Chapter 3. After treatment with antibiotics the use of papaya juice will quickly assist the restoration of the normal bacteria in the gut which will have been destroyed by the treatment. Papaya is good for many digestive disorders and is excellent for improving poor digestion. Therapeutically it can often be combined with pineapple juice in which there is another important enzyme, bromelain.

The skin of the papaya is a first class external treatment for skin wounds and places that do not heal quickly. The pulp from the juicer can be used for this and as a poultice.

PARSLEY
Carum petroselinum
Petroselinum sativum

Parsley is perhaps one of the most commonly used but therapeutically under-rated of herbs. How often one sees a dish in a restaurant garnished with parsley, and the waiter leaves the parsley on the serving dish or the customer rejects it as mere decoration.

Parsley contains more vitamin C than any other standard culinary vegetable, three times as much as oranges and rather more than blackcurrants. It is also one of the best providers of pro vitamin A with about as much as carrots. The iron content is high and the plant is a good source of manganese.

In the Middle Ages parsley was used for many conditions including 'fastening teeth' (because scurvy which is caused by a deficiency of vitamin C makes the gums spongy and the teeth loose) and for 'brightening dim eyes' (bad eyesight is a sign of shortage of vitamin A). The old herbalists often had good results without their knowing the chemistry involved.

The old Greeks were in awe of parsley because the herb was associated with Archemorus who was eaten by a serpent having been put on a parsley leaf as a baby by his careless nurse. Henceforward he became the harbinger of death.

On the bright side, they decorated the heroes of the Isthmian games with parsley garlands and decorated the many maidens that sang at feasts in the same way. This last use may be associated with the great effectiveness of parsley in increasing menstruation and assisting regularization of the monthly periods.

This action is due to the presence of apiol which is a constituent of the female sex hormone oestrogen. When this was discovered in 1849 the plant was used against the effects of malaria with some success. Father Kniepp said the plant was one of the most proven of all remedies as a diuretic to cure water retention or dropsy.

Today parsley is a valuable therapy for kidney stones, as a diuretic, for rheumatism, menstrual insufficiency and as a general stimulant. It settles the stomach and improves the appetite. The high contents of vitamins C and A and iron make parsley an important part of treatment for conditions associated with shortages of these important nutrients.

Parsley juice, being a herbal drink, is quite powerful and is usually taken in quantities of about 2 fl.oz. (50ml) three times a day and is best mixed with other juices. The leaves can be deep frozen and are easily stored. It is a good idea to use parsley in cooking as well as in the form of juice. Dried parsley is not a very satisfactory alternative to fresh and has a coarser flavour.

PINEAPPLE
Ananas sativus

Pineapple contains the protein digesting enzyme mixture called bromelain. The uses of these enzymes are mentioned in the notes on papaya and in Chapter 3, with regard to cancer. However, fresh pineapple juice has many other uses. When tuberculosis was common instead of the rarity it has now become, the juice was found to be effective in dissolving mucus and aiding recovery from the once dread disease.

Pineapple has been thought good for heart conditions and indeed should not be used by people with haemophilia or by those with diseases of the kidneys and liver. This is because it seems to reduce the time taken to coagulate the blood – which is why it can be useful for heart patients.

The Lancet has carried a paper by Dr S.L.B. Duncan in which he remained unconvinced of the beneficial results to be obtained on the mucus but believed it could be useful for women suffering from painful periods. It could be that the juice he used was not fresh, for many have attested to its value as a solvent of mucus. Probably more research is needed.

As pineapples are available in the winter they are useful as providers of vitamin C but, like apples, there can be a variation, said to range from 24-165mg in 100g. Canning or bottling divides these figures by three. Fresh is best by far.

Sore throats and bronchitis are relieved by sipping the juice. Choose ripe fruits of good colour for pineapples do not become sweeter on storage if they are picked green. This is because the starch in the stem is taken up into the fruit and converted to sugar only at the final stage of ripening. If it is cut off beforehand then the sweetness can be as little as a half of that found in a ripe fruit allowed to finish its development on the plant.

POTATO
Solanum tuberosum

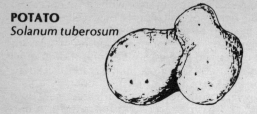

In about 1565 the Irish became the first nation to grow potatoes in Europe on a large scale. Some years before that Pisarro found them being cultivated, and also stored, by the Incas of Peru. Since then it has become the most widely grown vegetable in the Western world.

It is not true that potatoes are very fattening, they contain only about 20% carbohydrate. If you fry them the calorie count is more than trebled, but as the most important nutrients of the potato lie just under the skin the healthy way to eat them is baked or boiled after being scrubbed but not peeled.

In the winter the potato is one of the most useful sources of vitamin C, containing 20-30 mg per 100g (one medium potato). This is only reduced by 20-25% when cooked in the skin but by up to 50% otherwise.

It is important to remove any green from potatoes, they should be stored in the dark to lessen the possibility of this happening, and to cut any shoots that appear deeply away. This is because the green part of potatoes contains a toxic alkaloid called solanine. This is the same poison as is found in woody nightshade, which (like deadly nightshade which contains a different alkaloid, atropine) belongs to the same family as the potato, the *Solanaceae*.

Do not allow this to detract from the potatoes many merits, for the green colouring is easy to see and to remove. The tuber is a rich source of potassium containing some $2\frac{1}{2}$g of the mineral in 450g and there are valuable amounts of a number of the B vitamins.

Raw potato has a nutty flavour which is quite nice, although some people find the starch somewhat indigestible in this form. The juice is perfectly palatable but is much improved both in effect and in taste by being combined, especially with lemon or with carrot juice.

There have been several reports of excellent results from potato juice in cases of eczema. But remember that this complaint can arise for many different reasons including allergies and nerves, so the control of eczema is often difficult and requires much careful experimentation on the part of patient and practitioner.

The juice is very soothing on the gastric tract, so is used for duodenal and gastric ulcers and for gastritis. It also relieves constipation and helps haemorrhoids.

Used externally the juice is well known for clearing minor infections and blemishes of the skin. The author has successfully used the potato as did the 'white witches' in the middle ages, to cure warts. The method is to rub the wart hard with a freshly cut potato, and to bury it in the earth, telling the sufferer that as the potato rots away so will the warts fade and disappear. This method has proved completely effective on warts of long standing that caused great misery and embarrassment to young children. Perhaps the juice would work just as well, who knows?

PUMPKIN
Cucurbita pepo

The pumpkin is related to the squash, the courgette and the Italian zucchini. For centuries the Balkan peasants have used pumpkin seeds to help the prostate survive into old age and to preserve virility. When you use pumpkins for juice, the whole is employed including the seeds which contain 40% of a valuable oil.

The Spanish returning from America brought back pumpkins as a staple food of the American Indians worth cultivating in Europe. This easy-growing plant soon spread across the whole of southern Europe whilst in its native land it is made into pumpkin pie on Thanksgiving Day to recall the first festival given by the Pilgrim Fathers to celebrate the gathering in of the harvest.

It is likely that any member of the pumpkin family, including the melon and the marrow, will have a similar effect when the juice is used therapeutically. The use to which it has often been put with very beneficial results is as an anti-helmintic, or remover of worms from the digestive tract.

The kidneys are stimulated gently by the juice and water retention is reduced without any unpleasant side effects. The urine remains, or is helped to become, normal.

It seems certain that the seeds are an essential part of the juice, in fact they are sometimes used alone after having been pulverized. Nevertheless, the complete pumpkin, which is quite rich in vitamin C, is a rather neglected food. It is often used as a decoration rather than a dinner, and is worth more serious consideration as a food.

RHUBARB
Rheum palmatum
et japonicum

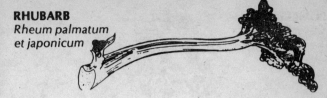

The rhubarb is an important medicinal herb in the treatment of constipation and, because of its astringent effect, in diarrhoea.

It should only be used occasionally, however, since the disadvantage is that, unlike spinach, it has few vitamins and minerals to offset its very high oxalic acid content. Oxalic acid combines with calcium to form crystals of insoluble calcium oxalate rendering it unusable by the body.

Rhubarb greens are even worse, and when it was suggested that they be used instead of spinach during the first world war some deaths were reported because of the coma resulting from oxalic acid poisoning.

Rhubarb is very rich in calcium but this is not, for the reasons given, available to the body.

SPINACH
Spinacia oleracea

Spinach is not only a famous vegetable but a very important remedy. It is one of the best ways of dealing with constipation. Roughage, especially in the form of cereal fibre, is an essential part of any natural diet and this is usually enough to relieve the trouble, but where this is not effective, raw spinach juice, in the absence of any serious disease, does the trick.

Because spinach is one of the best concentrators of valuable minerals and vitamins in all nature, the juice has an important role to play in building the blood and revitalizing the constitution. There is a high oxalic acid content which has the potential threat of being deposited as stones in the kidneys. Natural healers have, however, discovered that this complication never seems to occur when the *raw* juice is used. It can only result from a very excessive intake of cooked spinach.

Dr Ernst Meyer has drawn a significant parallel between the minerals in spinach and milk. He gives the following table:

	spinach	milk
Potassium	17.05	17.35
Sodium	36.30	7.00
Calcium	12.25	17.30
Magnesium	3.45	1.90
Iron	3.46	0.33
Phosphates	10.58	26.00
Sulphates	7.11	0 05
Chlorides	5.39	15.60

Dr Meyer makes the point that spinach is wonderfully suitable for the building of the blood, and that it not only contains a lot of the vital salts of iron and manganese, but also present is that rare component of the regeneration of the blood, cobalt. He concludes that spinach juice is the most important plant for the blood.

Spinach is rich in vitamins, containing almost as much carotene (pro vitamin A) as young carrots, much thiamine, riboflavin and nicotinic acid, as much vitamin C as oranges, and more folic acid than any culinary vegetable except asparagus.

Spinach juice should be used to aid recovery during the complaints of childhood and by all convalescents. Rheumatic sufferers claim benefit as do those with too little vitamin C in their diets. Spinach helps the nutrition of both expectant and nursing mothers and improves the quality of their milk.

The best quality juice requires a time between harvesting and pressing of not more than two hours. The resulting juice can then be deep-frozen or pasteurized and put into bottles for storage.

TOMATO
*Lycopersicum
esculentum*

Like tobacco and the potato, it was the conquest of the New World that brought the tomato to Europe. The plant originated in Peru, and when it was brought back it was admired to the extent that in Germany it was called the apple of paradise, and in England, the love apple.

The spread of the plant throughout the rest of the world took place in little more than a hundred years, and everywhere it was grown farmers were able to breed individual and interesting varieties to suit the local palate.

Often, especially in bad years, tomatoes are gathered green and allowed to ripen afterwards. This may be unavoidable but typical figures show that green tomatoes have a vitamin C content when ripe of about 29mg per 100g, whereas tomatoes picked ripe from the same plant contain 42mg per 100g. There is also some loss of carotene. Fresh ripe tomatoes are best.

Besides containing carotene and vitamin C the tomato is a good provider of the B vitamins and even contains some of the vitamins D, E and P. The minerals are also in profusion, including the trace elements cobalt and copper, as well as manganese, calcium, iron and phosphorus.

The therapeutic action of tomato juice is very mild but positive. The manganese helps the digestion and the well-balanced content of vital elements is good for the blood. It is an ideal children's health drink whilst being a first rate supportive therapy for any general debility or digestive upset.

Cooking quite alters the taste and reduces the value of the juice, so canned tomato juice, although in no way bad for you, is not to be compared to the freshly expressed nectar of ripe fruit.

A mixture of carrot, spinach and tomato juices is frequently used for anaemic conditions. It is particularly effective for little children who find the fine flavour of such a mixture an easy way of taking organic iron in amounts sufficient to bring benefits to their health.

TURNIP
Brassica rapa

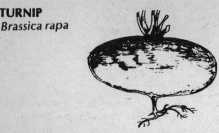

It is the turnip tops that have the most value in juice therapy, so be sure to buy your turnips complete. The root is delicious *sautéed* in a little oil, and in a stew it acts as a splendid rounder of flavours which it absorbs better than many other vegetables. The raw root cut into sticks, is good in salads or can be used for dips.

The tops are often recommended as a source of calcium, along with cabbage, spinach and watercress. The raw tops contain a great concentration of vitamin C, 120 mg in 100g. Cooking reduces this to only 40% but the calcium is not much altered.

The juice of the turnip makes a good general pick-me-up when you are a little run down or depressed, and is also good for the kidneys, and especially for stones.

When used with a properly based diet of raw fruits and vegetables for eight weeks, a blend of turnip leaves with equal amounts of watercress, spinach and carrot has been found effective in reducing haemorrhoids.

There is a slight expectorant effect which makes the juice helpful for chesty coughs and for bronchitis. In this case it combines well with lemon juice and, like the lemon, also has a bactericidal action.

Calcium is important for the teeth and bones of growing children, and, as turnip greens do not have much oxalic acid content they are a better source of this important mineral for the young. Although there is some likelihood that the oxalic acid found, for example, in spinach does not combine with and prevent the calcium from being used by the body when the vegetable is raw, turnip tops are better than spinach for very little children.

WATERCRESS
Nasturtium officinale

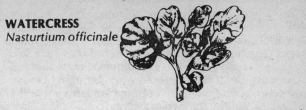

The watercress is second only to horseradish as a provider of sulphur. It is also rich in sodium, calcium, potassium, iron and the chlorides. Among the vitamins it contains are valuable amounts of folic acid, biotin, pantothenic acid, nicotinic acid and thiamine. Watercress is a plentiful source of vitamin A, by way of carotene, and of vitamin C. In addition it has been discovered that it is one of the best vegetable sources of the element iodine which is very important to the correct functioning of the thyroid gland.

In olden times writers like Xenophon spoke of the great revitalizing powers of watercress. Later on it was used for the digestive system and for the gallbladder and liver. In recent times, the discovery of the great restorative virtues of the plant as a purifier and strengthener of the blood have given it a special place in raw juice therapy.

Every spring it is good to take watercress juice diluted with five times as much spring water – about one dessertspoonful eight times a day for two weeks. This sets you up to take full physical advantage of the summer ahead.

The juice is too strong to take without dilution but mixes well with others, when it not only imparts an agreeable peppery flavour but also adds its own particular merits. For example, with cucumber and beet it helps remove the uric acid of rheumatism. With turnip tops, carrot and spinach it is good for anaemia and also, with turnip roots, to clear the coagulations of piles and similar growths. For this to be effective it is necessary to rigorously exclude refined foods from the diet and to continue with the treatment for up to six months.

Its mixture with carrot, parsley and potato juice is helpful in clearing the lungs and has brought relief to some sufferers from emphysema.

Watercress grows best in very pure, slowly running water, and used to be a common sight. Sadly, pollution has made it rarer than before, so usually it needs to be bought. The leaves are more tender than they look and wilt easily. Left dry, watercress becomes yellow within five or six hours, but it can be stored when brought home in good green condition in the bottom compartment of the refrigerator, lightly wrapped in a plastic bag.

CHAPTER 7

THERAPEUTIC INDEX

It is usually misleading to diagnose your own condition unless it be very simple and straightforward such as a non-persistent headache or acne. This book does not set out to help you discover what is wrong, but to aid you in restoring the organism to normality with vitality.

There are many good books available giving excellent advice on a correct and health giving diet. Raw juice therapy should always be used in conjunction with a sensible, natural diet, the precise composition of which is a matter for individual trial and experimentation. But every day you should have some whole grains, such as are in 100% wholewheat bread or unpolished rice and you should avoid refined, highly processed or so-called 'convenience' foods.

Do not allow good eating habits to make you a food bore. Unless you are on a very special diet for good medical reasons it is far better to accept a friend's misguided but well-meaning hospitality than to cause offence by refusal. Obviously vegetarians would make sure that their preferences were known – but it is easy to prepare unhealthy vegetarian food too! Your philosophy can be that it is vital to eat enough of the right foods so that the occasional indiscretions are nothing that a well-nourished body cannot take in its stride.

The quantities of juices given are to be taken over each day. Store under refrigeration until required. Where several formulae are given you may ring the changes depending on your personal preferences and the availability of the raw materials. Read the sections on each juice source before using the juices.

When it is not possible to prepare fresh juices use frozen or bottled and pasteurized products from manufacturers of repute.

Acne

Cut down consumption of fats, cream, chocolate and milk (except skimmed milk).

Carrot 16 fl.oz. (450ml) *plus* one of the following:
Carrot 6 fl.oz. (175ml); spinach 6 fl.oz. (175ml); lettuce 4 fl.oz. (100ml).
Carrot 10 fl.oz. (275ml); spinach 6 fl.oz. (175ml).
Asparagus 6 fl.oz. (175ml).

Adenoids

A complaint surgically operated upon far too often:

Carrot 16 fl.oz. (450ml) *plus* one of the following:
Horseradish (grated) 1oz. (25g); comfrey 10 fl.oz. (275ml).
Horseradish (grated) 1oz. (25g); garlic $\frac{1}{2}$ fl.oz. (15ml); onion 6 fl.oz. (175ml).

Allergies

Sensitivities to various substances, or even sunlight can give rise to allergic conditions. The first thing to do is to find the cause and try to avoid contact with it. The following juices are not so much remedies but rather for general strengthening:

Carrot 8 fl.oz. (225ml); beet (root only). 8 fl.oz. (225ml); beet (root only) 8 fl.oz. (225ml).
Artichoke (or elixir – *see page* 51) 2 fl.oz. (50ml); celery 10 fl.oz. (275ml)
Carrot 12 fl.oz. (350ml); celery 4 fl.oz. (100ml).
Carrot 8 fl.oz. (225ml); potato 8 fl.oz. (225ml).

Take any *two* of the above combinations daily.

Anaemia

Not pernicious anaemia, which must be treated by a physician, but simple anaemia as often occurs with women of child bearing age.

Take any two of the following:
Watercress 2 fl.oz. (50ml); horseradish (grated) 1 fl.oz. (25ml); spinach 12 fl.oz. (350ml).
Carrot 10 fl.oz. (275ml); spinach 6 fl.oz. (175ml).
Carrot 6 fl.oz. (175ml); fennel 6 fl.oz. (175ml); beetroot 6 fl.oz. (175ml).

Fennel 8 fl.oz. (225ml); Carrot 6 fl.oz. (175ml); spinach 2 fl.oz. (50ml).

Carrot 6 fl.oz. (175ml); beetroot 10 fl.oz. (275ml).

Fennel 8 fl.oz. (225ml); beetroot 8 fl.oz. (225ml).

Turnip tops 4 fl.oz. (100ml); carrot 4 fl.oz. (100ml); spinach 6 fl.oz. (175ml); watercress 2 fl.oz. (50ml).

Turnip tops 8 fl.oz. (225ml); watercress 3 fl.oz. (75ml); spinach 5 fl.oz. (150ml).

Watercress 3 fl.oz. (75ml); carrot 8 fl.oz. (225ml); beetroot 5 fl.oz. (150ml).

Nettle 10 fl.oz. (275ml); watercress 2 fl.oz. (50ml); beetroot 4 fl.oz. (100ml).

Tomato 7 fl.oz. (200ml) carrot 4 fl.oz. (100ml); spinach 5 fl.oz. (150ml).

On page 36 there is a list of foods rich in iron – be sure to include as many as you can in your diet.

Angina Pectoris

As a supportive measure raw juices can be helpful. Cut down on stressful situations, avoid all hardened fats, keep weight down to normal, take gentle regular exercise. Take one to three from the following:

Pineapple 10 fl.oz. (275ml); papaya 6 fl.oz. (175ml).

Garlic 1 fl.oz. (25ml); onion 8 fl.oz. (225ml); parsley 3 fl.oz. (75ml). orange 4 fl.oz. (100ml).

Garlic 1 fl.oz. (25ml); orange 10 fl.oz. (275ml); pineapple 5 fl.oz. (150ml).

Horseradish (grated) 1oz. (25g); carrot 15 fl.oz. (425ml).

Antibiotics

Sometimes in an emergency the doctor has to give antibiotics as a health saving measure, but they should never be given lightly for minor complaints.

Antibiotics destroy good and bad bacteria without discrimination. It is therefore necessary to re-establish a good gastric flora after any antibiotic treatment.

These are recommended:

Apple 10 fl.oz. (275ml).

Cucumber 10 fl.oz. (275ml); garlic 1 fl.oz. (25ml).

Onion 10 fl.oz. (275ml); garlic $\frac{1}{2}$ fl.oz. (15ml).

Papaya 16 fl.oz. (450ml).

Take daily, natural yogurt.

Arteries (Arteriosclerosis)
Keep your weight right. Use a diet rich in polyunsaturated oils and low in hard fats. Exercise gently and regularly – swimming or jogging are suitable. Vitamin E, 500mg a day, is thought by many to be valuable. Do not eat more than one egg each week. Avoid sugar and refined foods.

Take one from each group every day.

Group A
   Carrot 10 fl.oz. (275ml); spinach 6 fl.oz. (175ml).
   Carrot 8 fl.oz. (225ml); celery 4 fl.oz. (100ml); beetroot 4 fl.oz. (100ml).
   Carrot 8 fl.oz. (225ml); celery 4 fl.oz. (100ml); spinach 2 fl.oz. (50ml); parsley 2 fl.oz. (50ml).
   Carrot 8 fl.oz. (225ml); nettle 8 fl.oz. (225ml).

Group B
   Pineapple 6 fl.oz. (175ml); garlic 2 fl.oz. (50ml); carrot 8 fl.oz. (225ml).
   Pineapple 10 fl.oz. (275ml); papaya 6 fl.oz. (175ml).
   Pineapple 16 fl.oz. (450ml).
   Papaya 16 fl.oz. (450ml).

Group C
   Horseradish (grated) 1oz. (25g).
   Garlic 2 fl.oz. (50ml).

Arthritis
Once bone changes have occurred it is not possible to reverse them. Because of this it is surprising how many people successfully seek and find relief from arthritis through natural remedies. The fact is that mobility is often restored through the help of a sympathetic doctor well versed in the healing powers of plants.

Take as much celery and celery juice as you can – 2 pints a day is ideal. The celery should be used with one or more of the following:
   Cucumber 10 fl.oz. (275ml); Nettles 6 fl.oz. (175ml).
   Grapefruit (if you can take it) 16 fl.oz. (450ml).
   Nettle 13 fl.oz. (375ml); parsley 3 fl.oz. (75ml).
   Spinach 8 fl.oz. (225ml); parsley 2 fl.oz. (50ml); cucumber or nettle 6 fl.oz. (175ml).

Cucumber 6 fl.oz. (175ml); beetroot 7 fl.oz. (200ml); watercress 3 fl.oz. (75ml).

Asthma
One in fifty in Britain suffer from this exhausting complaint which causes a nervous spasm of the bronchioles which fill with mucus. Sometimes the cause can be traced and avoided. Try each combination of juices for at least a full week when attacks are expected. If you find one that helps, then keep with it for as long as remains useful:

Grapefruit 1pt. (550ml).
Carrot 10 fl.oz. (275ml); celery 10 fl.oz. (275ml).
Carrot 12 fl.oz. (350ml); spinach 8 fl.oz. (225ml).
Horseradish (grated) 4oz. (100g); lemon 4 fl.oz. (100ml); water 12 fl.oz. (350ml).
Carrot 13 fl.oz. (375ml); radish (root and top) 7 fl.oz. (200ml).
Lettuce 8 fl.oz. (225ml); celery 12 fl.oz. (350ml).
Lettuce 12 fl.oz. (350ml); potato 8 fl.oz. (225ml).
Carrot 5 fl.oz. (150ml); watercress 5 fl.oz. (150ml); parsley 3 fl.oz. (75ml); potato 7 fl.oz. (200ml).
Garlic 1 fl.oz. (25ml) each day.

Bad Breath
Check that your teeth are clean and without decay. Take bran to keep the bowels active. Ensure that any infections of the chest, nose, mouth and throat are treated.

Lemon juice 2 fl.oz. (50ml) in warm water on rising, *plus* one of:

Carrot 10 fl.oz. (275ml); spinach 5 fl.oz. (150ml); cucumber 5 fl.oz. (150ml).
Apple 1pt. (550ml).
Apple 10 fl.oz. (275ml); celery 8 fl.oz. (225ml).
Carrot 10 fl.oz. (275ml); celery 6 fl.oz. (175ml).

Bilious Attacks
Not vomiting, which see, but a failure to produce enough bile to digest the fats you have eaten. Cut down on all fats straight away. Do not drink alcohol and take one of the following:

Cucumber 4 fl.oz. (100ml); carrot 8 fl.oz. (225ml); beetroot 6 fl.oz. (175ml).
Carrot 10 fl.oz. (275ml); spinach 6 fl.oz. (175ml).
Carrot 10 fl.oz. (275ml); celery 6 fl.oz. (175ml); parsley 2 fl.oz. (50ml).
Dandelion 8 fl.oz. (225ml); watercress 4 fl.oz. (100ml); nettle 6 fl.oz. (175ml).

Blood, Purification

As the blood carries nutrients so it also takes away toxins. If this is not happening as efficiently as it should then certain raw juices are great stimulants to the improvement of the blood. Try one of the following:

Apple 16 fl.oz. (450ml).
Beetroot 16 fl.oz. (450ml).
Asparagus 2 fl.oz. (50ml) three times a day.
Beet 8 fl.oz. (225ml) three times a day.
Beet 8 fl.oz. (225ml); cucumber 6 fl.oz. (175ml); carrot 6 fl.oz. (175ml).
Nettle 4 fl.oz. (100ml); beet 6 fl.oz. (175ml).
Spinach 8 fl.oz. (225ml); beetroot 8 fl.oz. (225ml).
Watercress 4 fl.oz. (100ml); carrot 12 fl.oz. (350ml).

Boils, Abcesses etc

Usually the outward sign of inner toxic waste. Keep very clean and be sure your diet is right with plenty of fresh, uncooked fruit and vegetables and wholewheat bread. Use papaya pulp as an external poultice or, failing that, pure honey. Use one or two of the following:

Carrot 7 fl.oz. (200ml); beetroot and tops 10 fl.oz. (275ml); garlic 1 fl.oz. (25ml).
Onion 5 fl.oz. (150ml); cabbage 15 fl.oz. (425ml).
Watercress 5 fl.oz. (150ml); nettle 5 fl.oz. (150ml); cabbage 10 fl.oz. (275ml).
Garlic 2 fl.oz. (50ml); onion 5 fl.oz. (150ml); beetroot and tops 9 fl.oz. (250ml).

Bones and Teeth

For both children and old people there is a need for plenty of calcium as this mineral is not usually well absorbed. Make juices from any of the calcium rich foods in the list on page 38. Drink at least a pint a day.

Among the best are celery, parsley and watercress. Spinach contains oxalic acid and it is possible that this combines with the calcium rendering it useless, although some authorities claim that this is not true of the raw juice.

Bronchitis

Try to give up smoking. If you can, move to a high location with very clean fresh air. Keep your weight down. To shift the mucus take, every day, for at least two months:

Horseradish (grated) 4oz. (100g); juice of 2 lemons in 12 fl.oz. (350ml) water. *And/or*:

Onion 10 fl.oz. (275ml).

Turnip 10 fl.oz. (275ml); lemon 4 fl.oz. (100ml).

As an internal disinfectant take daily:

Cabbage 18 fl.oz. (500ml); garlic 2 fl.oz. (50ml).

And to restore strength:

Carrot 12 fl.oz. (350ml); Dandelion 5 fl.oz. (150ml). *Or*:

Carrot 10 fl.oz. (275ml); beetroot and tops 5 fl.oz. (150ml); cucumber 5 fl.oz. (150ml).

To clear the throat use pineapple juice, 16 fl.oz. (450ml).

Cancer

An overall name for a variety of malignant conditions. Always see a practitioner. Read the section on cancer in this book. Raw juices can provide a valuable and nourishing support for any treatment that your physician feels is suitable. Cancer is frequently controlled nowadays so try to be positive and not pessimistic.

Carrot 2pt. (1l) a day. *Or*:

Beetroot 2pt. (1l) a day. *Or*:

Carrot 1pt. (550ml); beetroot 1 pt. (550ml). *Plus*:

Apricot kernels, 20 a day.

Papaya 1pt. (550ml) a day.

Cataracts

Needs skilled medical advice but if dealt with early can respond to natural methods. Select one of the following:

Carrot 10 fl.oz. (275ml); celery 5 fl.oz. (150ml); parsley 3 fl.oz. (75ml); watercress 2 fl.oz. (50ml).

Carrot 6 fl.oz. (175ml); beet 5 fl.oz. (150ml); cucumber 5 fl.oz. (150ml).

Carrot 10 fl.oz. (275ml); parsley 3 fl.oz. (75ml); spinach 3 fl.oz. (75ml).

Carrot 8 fl.oz. (225ml); watercress 5 fl.oz. (150ml); tomato 7 fl.oz. (200ml).

Catarrh

Cut out smoking and all refined foods. Remedy any overweight.

Garlic (1 fl.oz./25ml per day) is effective in many cases. The following are also most helpful:

Juice of 2 lemons; Horseradish (grated) 4 fl.oz. (100ml); warm water 12 fl.oz. (350ml).

Carrot 12 fl.oz. (350ml); spinach 4 fl.oz. (100ml).

Carrot 10 fl.oz. (275ml); celery 10 fl.oz. (275ml).

Carrot 6 fl.oz. (175ml); celery 6 fl.oz. (175ml); radish 4 fl.oz. (100ml).

Carrot 5 fl.oz. (150ml); beetroot 7 fl.oz. (200ml); cucumber 4 fl.oz. (100ml).

Carrot 10 fl.oz. (275ml); radish 4 fl.oz. (100ml); parsley 2 fl.oz. (50ml).

Papaya 10 fl.oz. (275ml); pineapple 5 fl.oz. (150ml); grapefruit 5 fl.oz. (150ml).

Onion 10 fl.oz. (275ml).

Circulation

To help circulation take regular exercise.

The juices to use are:

Horseradish (grated) 4oz. (100g).

Carrot 10 fl.oz. (275ml).

Colds

Massive doses (1-2 grams every three hours) of vitamin C (at onset of symptoms). If you can find it, 10mg Propolis (the resinous cement from beehives) is most useful, taken three times a day. Hot lemon juice is soothing, otherwise treatment as for catarrh. As a specific, orange juice 1pt (500ml) is a good idea.

Colitis

Take plenty of bran and cereal roughage in the diet. The bland meals which used to be recommended are not usually helpful. Take the juice of a lemon in warm water on rising *plus*:

Apple 10 fl.oz. (275ml); carrot 8 fl.oz. (225ml). *Or*:

Cucumber 6 fl.oz. (175ml); carrot 5 fl.oz. (150ml); beetroot 9 fl.oz. (250ml).

Papaya 1pt. (500ml) is recommended as available.

Constipation

Make sure your diet has enough roughage from wholewheat that is preferably stoneground. Two tablespoonsful of blackstrap molasses in warm water shifts most people's difficult problems without strain. Yogurt is also to be recommended, but make sure that it is free from synthetic colours and flavourings. The following can be used individually, or together:

Spinach 16 fl.oz. (450ml).

Carrot 10 fl.oz. (275ml); spinach 6 fl.oz. (175ml).

Carrot 8 fl.oz. (225ml); apple 10 fl.oz. (275ml).

Potato 12 fl.oz. (350ml).

Convalescence

A time to rebuild your health with exercise and fresh air. The juices can be chosen from one or more of these:

Beetroot 12 fl.oz. (350ml); carrot 6 fl.oz. (175ml); parsley 2 fl.oz. (50ml).

Fennel 6 fl.oz. (175ml); carrot 8 fl.oz. (225ml).

French or string beans 5 fl.oz. (150ml).

Coronary Thrombosis

Always to be treated in the closest co-operation with your physician. No smoking, cut down stressful occupations. Take gentle, regular exercise as soon as this is permitted. Remedy any overweight. Make sure that the majority of the fat consumed is polyunsaturated such as corn oil. Take daily:

Garlic 1 fl.oz. (25ml); carrot 7 fl.oz. (200ml). *And/or*:

Horseradish (grated) 2oz. (50g); Juice of 2 lemons; Warm water 12 fl.oz. (350ml). *Plus* any one of:

Carrot 8 fl.oz. (225ml); parsley 2 fl.oz. (50ml).
Carrot 6 fl.oz. (175ml); beetroot 7 fl.oz. (200ml); cucumber 5fl.oz. (150ml).
Pineapple 1pt. (500ml).
Papaya 1pt. (500ml).

Coughing

A cough which is expectorant, i.e. productive in removing mucus, is a necessary protective mechanism. Dry coughs are eased by gargling with and then swallowing:

Juice of 2 lemons; 2 tablespoonsful honey, warm water 5 fl.oz. (150ml).

Find the cause of the cough, for example a cold or catarrh, and then treat the condition. Avoid smokey atmospheres. A good treatment is:

Onion 10 fl.oz. (275ml) each day.

Dermatitis

If caused by an outside irritant, remove the cause. Try spreading on either avocado pulp or papaya pulp.

In rare cases this is due to Vitamin A deficiency. If so take any of the following:

Carrot 6 fl.oz. (175ml); apple 6 fl.oz. (175ml); celery 6 fl.oz. (175ml).
Carrot 10 fl.oz. (275ml); celery 6 fl.oz. (175ml).
Parsley 2 fl.oz. (50ml); watercress 3 fl.oz. (75ml); carrot 11 fl.oz. (300ml).

Diabetes

Should invariably be treated by an experienced physician for if the condition is well controlled the sufferer can expect a relatively normal life.

Several very helpful and low-carbohydrate juice combinations have been found useful especially for the type of diabetes that begins in adult life. One of the best is:

Brussels sprouts 10 fl.oz. (275ml); runner or string beans 10 fl.oz. (275ml).

Another good mixture is:

Horseradish (grated) 3oz. (75g); juice of 2 lemons;

water 10 fl.oz. (275ml).
Others to try include:
Carrot 8 fl.oz. (225ml); spinach 8 fl.oz. (225ml).
Carrot 12 fl.oz. (350ml); celery 2 fl.oz. (50ml); parsley 2 fl.oz. (50ml).
Lettuce 6 fl.oz. (175ml); runner bean 7 fl.oz. (200ml); brussels sprout 7 fl.oz. (200ml).

Diarrhoea
If persistent, consult a physician. There are several good juice combinations for diarrhoea, use any of them:
Beetroot 16 fl.oz. (450ml).
Cabbage 16 fl.oz. (450ml).
Beetroot 8 fl.oz. (225ml); cabbage 8 fl.oz. (225ml).
Garlic 2 fl.oz. (225ml); cabbage 8 fl. oz. (225ml).
Garlic 2 fl.oz. (50ml); beetroot 14 fl.oz. (400ml).
Nettle 16 fl.oz. (450ml).
Nettle 8 fl.oz. (225ml); garlic 1 fl.oz. (25ml); cabbage 7 fl.oz. (200ml).
Papaya 16 fl.oz. (450ml).
Papaya 8 fl.oz. (225ml); pineapple 8 fl.oz. (225ml).

Dropsy
See Water Retention

Dysentery
Treat as for diarrhoea, rest, take at least 5pt. (2½l) of fluid daily, ideally half in the form of a normal saline solution obtainable from most chemists.

Dyspepsia
See Indigestion.

Eczema
Not so much a disease as a symptom. Many causes including hereditary and sensitivity. Often brought on by stress and worry. Try to find and eliminate the cause. Take a non-stimulating diet. Vegetarianism is ideal. Try any of the following:
Spinach 5 fl.oz. (150ml); carrot 11 fl.oz. (300ml).

Carrot 6 fl.oz. (175ml); celery 6 fl.oz. (175ml); spinach 2 fl.oz. (50ml);
Parsley 2 fl.oz. (50ml).
Spinach 12 fl.oz. (350ml).
Lettuce 10 fl.oz. (275ml).
Papaya 16 fl.oz. (450ml).
Artichoke or elixir (see page 51) 6 fl.oz. (175ml).
Nettles 6 fl.oz. (175ml).
Potato 12 fl.oz. (350ml).

Emphysema

Needs to be treated by a physician. Reports indicate that some patients have been helped with:
Watercress 6 fl.oz. (175ml) a day. Or:
Watercress 6 fl.oz. (175ml); parsley 4 fl.oz. (100ml); potato 6 fl.oz. (175ml).

Eyes

Night blindness is a sign of vitamin A deficiency.

Use any of the vitamin A-rich juices, particularly good are the following:
Fennel 8 fl.oz. (225ml); carrot 8 fl.oz. (225ml).
Watercress 3 fl.oz. (75ml); parsley 1 fl.oz. (25ml); carrot 10 fl.oz. (275ml).
Papaya 16 fl.oz. (450ml).
Carrot 8 fl.oz. (225ml); celery 6 fl.oz. (175ml); spinach 2 fl.oz. (50ml).
Carrot 8 fl.oz. (225ml); celery 8 fl.oz. (225ml).
Carrot 10 fl.oz. (275ml); fennel 6 fl.oz. (175ml).

Fatigue

After hard work, fatigue is nature's way of telling you to rest, so rest. Overdoing it leaves the body weakened and vulnerable to disease.

If you are fatigued without hard work, either you need more sleep (needs vary widely), or you are not active enough, idleness is itself tiring; or you are ill, in which case the cause must be found and treated. Most likely of all, you need a nutritional 'pick-me-up'.

Take a two-week course of:

Watercress juice diluted with five times the volume of

spring water, 1 dessertspoonful eight times a day.
And/or:
Orange 8 fl.oz. (225ml); apple 8 fl.oz. (225ml); lemon 1
fl.oz. (25ml); lettuce 1 fl.oz. (25ml).

Fever

This condition is the natural response of the body in its
fight to destroy infections. Treat the cause. Drink juices to
suit you especially all citrus, grape and celery. Use garlic,
cabbage and onion juices to help fight the infection.

Fractures

To heal fractures the body must have an abundant supply
of vitamin C, protein and calcium.
    The best juice is:
    Comfrey 16 fl.oz. (450ml) each day.

Gallstones

Some doctors say that gallstones can only be cured by
surgery – and in some cases they are right. Good results
have been observed, though, with natural methods.
Avoid fatty foods and reduce weight to normal. Doctors
say that a typical patient is female, fat and forty!
    The following juice combinations are useful:
    Apple 10 fl.oz. (275ml); celery 6 fl.oz. (175ml).
    Beetroot 16 fl.oz. (450ml).
    Nettle 6 fl.oz. (175ml); watercress 4 fl.oz. (100ml).
    Carrot 6 fl.oz. (175ml); beetroot 5 fl.oz. (150ml);
    cucumber 5 fl.oz. (150ml).
Celery juice is particularly recommended for its effect in
preventing the formation of further gallstones.

Goitre

This enlargement of the thyroid gland is due to too little
iodine in the diet. Goitre is only common in areas with
little natural iodine where the usual preventative measure
or remedy is to use iodized table salt, or better still, sea
salt in cooking.
    The natural way is to add a teaspoonful of kelp or dulse
to one of the following combinations:

Parsley 1 fl.oz. (25ml); carrot 7 fl.oz. (200ml); celery 8 fl.oz. (225ml).
Carrot 10 fl.oz. (275ml); spinach 4 fl.oz. (100ml); watercress 2 fl.oz. (50ml).

Gout

This condition is very painful but happily not common. Cut down wine and beer and foods rich in nucleo-proteins such as anchovies or sardines. A vegetarian diet is best. Whisky is not conducive to gout so a drink is permissible.

The juice of choice is:

French or string beans 5 fl.oz. (150ml) a day.

Haemorrhoids (Piles)

These arise following pregnancy or through straining at the toilet. A diet rich in cereal fibre (bran) nearly always prevents piles from beginning and is essential for their relief. Sitting on radiators has not been proven as a cause.

Always check the diagnosis with your physician. Juices that help include:

Nettle 1 tablespoonful three times a day.

Potato 8 fl.oz. (225ml); watercress 8 fl.oz. (225ml).

Turnip tops 4 fl.oz. (100ml); watercress 4 fl.oz. (100ml); spinach 4 fl.oz. (100ml); carrot 4 fl.oz. (100ml).

Hair Loss

This is often an inherited condition about which nothing much can be done. None the less a daily rub of the scalp with nettle juice is said to help as is:

Spinach 10 fl.oz. (275ml); lettuce 10 fl.oz. (275ml) consumed daily for at least 6 months.

Read the article on lettuce before embarking on this method of restoring hair. Another juice combination is:

Alfalfa 6 fl.oz. (175ml); lettuce 4 fl.oz. (100ml); carrot 6 fl.oz. (175ml).

Hangover

It is doubted whether the readers of this book will be so indiscreet as to suffer from this condition themselves, none the less anyone may find it necessary to give treatment.

If you can, persuade the heavy drinker to take at least a pint, preferably two, of water before retiring to bed.

In the morning he will be suffering from vitamin B deficiency, vitamin C deficiency and a headache. Give:

2 tablespoonsful dried yeast, 4 tablespoonsful honey in 1 pt. (550ml) of citrus juice or papaya or pineapple juice.

Repeat every two hours.

Hay Fever

As with asthma (which see) hay fever is caused by a sensitivity to an outside influence which has to be located and, where possible, avoided. Children often grow out of hay fever and it often becomes much milder or non-existent as the years pass. Use any of these:

Celery 8 fl.oz. (225ml); carrot 12 fl.oz. (350ml).

Carrot 6 fl.oz. (175ml); beetroot 6 fl.oz. (175ml); cucumber 4 fl.oz. (100ml).

Carrot 8 fl.oz. (225ml); celery 3 fl.oz. (75ml); spinach 3 fl.oz. (75ml); parsley 2 fl.oz. (50ml).

Horseradish (grated) 3oz. (75g); juice of 2 lemons; water 12 fl.oz. (350ml).

Carrot 10 fl.oz. (275ml); spinach 6 fl.oz. (175ml).

Carrot 7 fl.oz. (200ml); beetroot 5 fl.oz. (150ml); lettuce 4 fl.oz. (100ml).

Headaches

A warning of strain on the body through stress or toxins. Prevention is better than cure. Persistent headaches can be a sign of disease and should always be referred to a physician. The remedy lies in treating the underlying cause. An eliminitive diet, rich in raw fruits and vegetables and whole grains is very useful. Try the following juice combinations:

Cabbage 12 fl.oz. (350ml); celery 4 fl.oz. (100ml).

Artichoke or elixir (see page 51) 2 fl.oz. (50ml) every 4 hours.

Apple 8 fl.oz. (225ml); tomato 8 fl.oz. (225ml); parsley 2 fl.oz. (50ml).

Beetroot 10 fl.oz. (275ml); cabbage 10 fl.oz. (275ml):
Beetroot 16 fl.oz. (450ml).
Carrot 10 fl.oz. (275ml); beet 4 fl.oz. (100ml); cucumber
6 fl.oz. (175ml).

Heart Trouble

Check with your physician. Ensure that your diet is rich in
polyunsaturates such as corn oil, take gentle exercise and
keep weight normal. Juices to help include:
Beetroot 16 fl.oz. (450ml).
Papaya 16 fl.oz. (450ml).
Pineapple 16 fl.oz. (450ml).
Pineapple 10 fl.oz. (275ml); papaya 6 fl.oz. (175ml).
Horseradish (grated) 4oz. (100g); garlic 1 fl.oz. (25ml); 2
lemons (juices); water 12 fl.oz. (350ml).
Carrot 6 fl.oz. (175ml); celery 5 fl.oz. (150ml); parsley 2
fl.oz. (50ml); spinach 3 fl.oz.

Hernia

This protrusion of a loop of gut through the wall of the
abdomen is caused by the strain thrown on man's body
by having adopted the practice of standing upright. Two
percent of British males have a hernia. Women have
inherently stronger abdominal muscles and are not so
likely to have a hernia.

Prevention consists of lifting heavy objects with the leg
muscles rather than the back or stomach muscles and
keeping the abdomen well exercised and the muscles in
good tone. The latter is aided by sound nutrition and the
following juices help here:
Carrot 6 fl.oz. (175ml); celery 5 fl.oz. (150ml); spinach 3
fl.oz. (75ml); parsley 2 fl.oz. (50ml).
Carrot 8 fl.oz. (225ml); celery 8 fl.oz. (225ml).
Carrot 12 fl.oz. (350ml); spinach 4 fl.oz. (100ml).
Carrot 10 fl.oz. (275ml); beet (tops and root) 3 fl.oz.
(75ml); cucumber 3 fl.oz. (75ml).

High Blood-Pressure

Your doctor should be seen regularly to check, advise
and to tell you if it is high enough to matter much. Do not
worry, do not smoke, do not take too much alcohol. Keep

weight moderate. Each day take 1 fl.oz. (25ml) garlic mixed with 7 fl.oz. (200ml) of carrot juice (see section on garlic). Also any of the following:

Carrot 8 fl.oz. (225ml); parsley 2 fl.oz. (50ml).
Carrot 6 fl.oz. (175ml); beetroot 7 fl.oz. (200ml); cucumber 5 fl.oz. (150ml).
Pineapple 1pt. (550ml).
Papaya 1pt. (550ml).
Alfalfa 10 fl.oz. (275ml); carrot 10 fl.oz. (275ml).
Orange 1pt. (550ml).

Indigestion

Caused by many different factors. Often not too much acid, but too much alkali in the system. The objective must be to normalize and not use the strong antacids commonly employed. Try these different juices until you find the right one for your indigestion. Give it two weeks before changing:

Cabbage 16 fl.oz. (450ml).
Papaya 16 fl.oz. (450ml).
Pineapple 16 fl.oz. (450ml).
Juice of 2 lemons in hot water with a little honey.
Carrot 6 fl.oz. (175ml); beetroot 7 fl.oz. (200ml); lettuce 3 fl.oz. (75ml).
Dandelion coffee (see section on dandelions) should replace ordinary beverages.

If due to anxiety use:

Beetroot 16 fl.oz. (450ml).

Tomato juice is very soothing.

Influenza (see colds)

Influenza is not to be taken lightly. Old people can even die from it as can the weak. It is good practice to begin winter with a good, nutritious course of juices lasting two weeks to build resistance. This can be repeated a week or so after Christmas. Take each day:

Watercress 3 fl.oz. (75ml); parsley 2 fl.oz. (50ml); carrot 7 fl.oz. (200ml); potato 7 fl.oz. (200ml).

If you catch influenza the one thing to avoid is anxiety about your sleeplessness because that just makes matters worse. Try an extra pillow or two to help breathing. Take

some exercise an hour before bedtime, even if only a
walk. On retiring drink a glass of your favourite warm
juice into which a tablespoonful of honey has been
dissolved. Lemon is often good. During the day drink one
of the following:

Celery 8 fl.oz. (225ml); carrot 8 fl.oz. (225ml).

In the evening rub on the brow:

Lettuce 1 fl.oz. (25ml); oil of roses 3 drops. And take:

Lettuce 4 fl.oz. (100ml).

Jaundice

Make sure that the diet is without alcohol and virtually
fat-free.

Carrot 8 fl.oz. (225ml); celery 5 fl.oz. (150ml); parsley 3
fl.oz. (75ml).

Watercress 2 fl.oz. (50ml); parsley 2 fl.oz. (50ml); nettles
12 fl.oz. (350ml).

Carrot 12 fl.oz. (350ml).

Kidneys

It is important to drink sufficient fluid every day. Here raw
juice therapy is most useful. Use one or more of the
following:

Artichoke or elixir (see page 51) 6 fl.oz. (175ml) each
day.

Asparagus 2 fl.oz. (50ml) three times a day.

Beetroot 8 fl.oz. (225ml); carrot 5 fl.oz. (150ml);
cucumber 3 fl.oz. (75ml).

Celery 6 fl.oz. (175ml); beetroot 6 fl.oz. (175ml);
cucumber 4 fl.oz. (100ml).

Laryngitis

Treat as for colds. Gargle with lemon juice diluted in
warm water.

The following juice combinations are used:

Carrot 8 fl.oz. (225ml); pineapple 8 fl.oz. (225ml).

Pineapple 16 fl.oz. (450ml).

Carrot 8 fl.oz. (225ml); apple 8 fl.oz. (225ml).

Carrot 6 fl.oz. (175ml); beetroot 5 fl.oz. (150ml);
cucumber 5 fl.oz. (150ml).

Liver
Trouble with the liver is often due to too much alcohol, too much fat and too few B vitamins. Take yeast supplementation. The following juices should be used two each day:

Carrot 6 fl.oz. (175ml); beetroot 5 fl.oz. (150ml); cucumber 5 fl.oz. (150ml).

Carrot 8 fl.oz. (225ml); celery 8 fl.oz. (225ml).

Spinach 5 fl.oz. (150ml); carrot 11 fl.oz. (300ml).

Carrot 9 fl.oz. (250ml); celery 5 fl.oz. (150ml); parsley 2 fl.oz. (50ml).

Apple 12 fl.oz. (350ml).

Artichoke or elixir (see page 51) 2 fl.oz. (50ml) three times a day.

Low Blood-Pressure
Usually an inconvenience but by no means a serious worry unless very low. Take one of the following:

Carrot 10 fl.oz. (275ml); spinach 6 fl.oz. (175ml).

Beetroot 12 fl.oz. (275ml); spinach 6 fl.oz. (175ml).

Parsley 3 fl.oz. (75ml); watercress 2 fl.oz. (50ml); carrot 6 fl.oz. (175ml); celery 5 fl.oz. (150ml).

Menstruation, Excessive
Take iron. Good juice combinations are:

Fennel 8 fl.oz. (225ml); beetroot 8 fl.oz. (225ml).

Nettle 8 fl.oz. (225ml); beetroot 8 fl.oz. (225ml).

See Anaemia.

Menstruation, Irregular
Parsley 6 fl.oz. (175ml) a day.

Migraine
A nervous contraction of the blood vessels in the brain can be caused by worry or by an allergy. Often the reason cannot be ascertained. The juice most in favour is fennel 12 fl.oz. (350ml).

Mucous Membranes
Dry mucous membranes are prone to infection so you need regular supplies of essential nutrients to maintain

them in good order. These are found in any two of the following:

Carrot 8 fl.oz. (225ml); apple 8 fl.oz. (225ml).

Carrot 8 fl.oz. (225ml); pineapple 8 fl.oz. (225ml).

Carrot 5 fl.oz. (150ml); beetroot 6 fl.oz. (175ml); cucumber 5 fl.oz. (150ml).

Horseradish (grated 2oz. (50g); lemon juice 1 fl.oz. (25ml); water 10 fl.oz. (275ml).

Nervous System

There are several powerful juices for helping the nervous system but before using them examine your lifestyle to shed unnecessary loads whilst you rebuild your health.

The following juices can be used to good effect:

Asparagus 2 fl.oz. (50ml); three times each day.

Dandelion 6 fl.oz. (175ml); nettle 4 fl.oz. (100ml).

Lettuce 3 fl.oz. (75ml); celery 6 fl.oz. (175ml); parsley 3 fl.oz. (75ml).

French or string beans, alone 16 fl.oz. (450ml), or with equal amounts of brussels sprout juice.

Nursing and Expectant Mothers

Take particular care to have enough of vitamins A, D, and C and of iron.

Have daily:

Carrot juice 10 fl.oz. (275ml); watercress 2 fl.oz. (50ml).

And one of the following:

Parsley 2 fl.oz. (50ml); tomato 12 fl.oz. (350ml).

Carrot 8 fl.oz. (225ml); Apple 8 fl.oz. (225ml).

Carrot 6 fl.oz. (175ml); beetroot 6 fl.oz. (175ml); cucumber 4 fl.oz. (100ml).

Carrot 8 fl.oz. (225ml); beetroot 8 fl.oz. (225ml).

Overweight

If, on checking the scales, you find that you are overweight, sip a glass of water with 2 teaspoonsful of cider vinegar or of lemon juice slowly during every meal, and drink nothing else with your food.

When hungry, on your calorie controlled diet (without one slimming is not likely), use juices to satisfy your craving for food. Choose from the following:

Carrot 8 fl.oz. (225ml); celery 8 fl.oz. (225ml).
Spinach 8 fl.oz. (225ml); beetroot 8 fl.oz. (225ml).
Cucumber 4 fl.oz. (100ml); beetroot 6 fl.oz. (175ml);
tomato 6 fl.oz. (175ml).
Or any others you fancy. A pre-meal mixture which helps
to reduce appetite is:
1 tablespoonful honey; celery 10 fl.oz. (275ml).

Peptic, Duodenal or Gastric Ulcers
Read the articles on cabbage and papaya. Do not take a
bland diet unless there is a special medical reason for
doing so. On the contrary, use wholemeal bread. Take
Cabbage 16 fl.oz. (450ml) – 30 fl.oz. (850ml) a day, and,
as desired;
Pineapple and papaya juice.
Comfrey 12 fl.oz. (350ml).
Potato 16 fl.oz. (450ml).

Pernicious Anaemia
To be treated by a physician. Vegans may be prone to
suffer and should therefore have regularly as a
preventative measure:
Comfrey 16 fl.oz. (450ml).

Pleurisy
Always to be treated and followed up by your
practitioner. Treat as for fever, but in convalescence you
need breathing exercises. Pineapple juice is particularly
good.

Pregnancy
See nursing and expectant mothers.

Prostate
An enlargement of the prostate gland is usually
manifested by frequent, rather slow, urination. A good
juice to use is:
Beetroot 16 fl.oz. (450ml).

Rejuvenation
Opinions are divided as to whether this is possible or

not. My opinion is that the prolongation of life in a well nourished person is unlikely but that an increase in the quality of that life is usually possible.

The usual, and valuable supportive substances are ginseng, pollen and Vitamin E. Besides that papaya, 16 fl.oz. (450ml) a day, is very useful.

Rheumatism, Muscular
(For other rheumatic conditions see under appropriate term). You need to build up strength and flush away toxic wastes. Use any of the following:

Celery 8 fl.oz. (225ml); carrot 8 fl.oz. (225ml).

Carrot 8 fl.oz. (225ml); orange 8 fl.oz. (225ml).

Carrot 6 fl.oz. (175ml); beetroot 6 fl.oz. (175ml); cucumber 4 fl.oz. (100ml).

Celery 6 fl.oz. (175ml); carrot 8 fl.oz. (225ml); cucumber 6 fl.oz. (175ml).

Watercress 4 fl.oz. (100ml); cucumber 4 fl.oz. (100ml); beetroot 8 fl.oz. (225ml).

Drink dandelion coffee instead of other beverages.

Sexual Drive – Excessive
A healthy love life of reasonable proportions often goes hand-in-hand with a long life, Sir Charles Chaplin and pianist Arthur Rubinstein being typical examples. But too great a sexual drive can be embarrassing and bad for normal social contact and friendship. Take:

Lettuce 10 fl.oz. (275ml) each day.

Sexual Drive – Lost or Weakened
Vitamin E, ginseng, honey and pollen are all said to aid lovemaking. There are also some good juices to use as well:

Beetroot 16 fl.oz. (450ml).

Beetroot 8 fl.oz. (225ml); carrot 8 fl.oz. (225ml); cucumber 6 fl.oz. (175ml).

Celery 12 fl.oz. (350ml).

Sinus Troubles
Can be very painful. Read articles on horseradish and garlic. For a basis of nutrients take:

Carrot 10 fl.oz. (275ml); pineapple or papaya 10 fl.oz. (275ml). *Plus*:
Horseradish (grated) 4oz. (100g); lemon 1 fl.oz. (25ml); radish (leaves and root) 6 fl.oz. (175ml); carrot 8 fl.oz. (225ml). *Plus*:
Garlic 1 fl.oz. (25ml) daily.

Skin – Poor Complexion
See Avocado article for helpful guidance. Papaya pulp helps remove blemishes. Lemon and cucumber juices are magnificent and effective cosmetics. Do not allow synthetics to clog the pores. Among the juices and juice combinations which improve the complexion are:
Apple 12 fl.oz. (350ml).
Beetroot 12 fl.oz. (350ml).

Spring Clean
Every spring give the body a chance to recover from the stresses of winter and to start afresh. Give yourself a vegetarian diet, low in refined starches and without added sugar, then take each day, for two weeks, one third before each meal:
Nettle 8 fl.oz. (225ml); watercress 6 fl.oz. (175ml); dandelion 6 fl.oz. (175ml).

Sunburn
High quantities of vitamin A and of calcium are helpful but the best idea is to prevent burning. To do this use the juice from the avocado as a sunscreening agent. Above all, be prudent and just expose your body for about fifteen minutes on the first day. Then you can double the exposure time every day, especially if you avoid the high burning times between 11.30am and 2.30pm.

Tonsils
Like adenoids, a favourite for unnecessary removal. Tonsils are important in the control of infection and should not be lost without due consideration.
The juices to use are:
Onion 8 fl.oz. (225ml); carrot 8 fl.oz. (225ml).
Horseradish (grated) 2oz. (50g); garlic 1 fl.oz. (25ml);

pineapple 13 fl.oz. (375ml). Plus any one of the following:

Carrot 8 fl.oz. (225ml); celery 8 fl.oz. (225ml).

Alfalfa 6 fl.oz. (175ml); celery 2 fl.oz. (50ml); carrot 8 fl.oz. (225ml).

Apple 8 fl.oz. (225ml); celery or carrot 8 fl.oz. (225ml).

Underweight

Not nearly so common as overweight and only rarely to be worried about. The trouble is that if the fat over the body is too thin then the insulation from extremes in temperature is poor. The remedy is to eat more. A good juice combination is:

Alfalfa 10 fl.oz. (275ml); carrot 10 fl.oz. (275ml).

Varicose Veins

Aggravated by the strains of constipation. Use whole cereals and take 8 fl.oz. (225ml) apple juice each day in the morning. Use also:

Asparagus 2 fl.oz. (50ml) three times a day.

Potato 12 fl.oz. (350ml) a day.

Vomiting

Being sick. If the cause is not apparent, seek medical advice. If caused through indiscreet eating and/or drinking rest is helpful with one of the following:

Papaya 12 fl.oz. (350ml).

Pineapple 12 fl.oz. (350ml).

Parsley 4 fl.oz. (100ml); tomato 10 fl.oz. (275ml).

Warts

Use 'magic'! (See section on potatoes).

Water Retention

Can result from various causes which should also be treated, such as poor circulation, kidney troubles and so on.

Juices with good diuretic (water passing) properties include:

Artichoke or elixir (see page 51) 6 fl.oz. (175ml) a day.

Asparagus 6 fl.oz. (175ml) a day.

Celery 16 fl.oz. (450ml).

Cucumber 8 fl.oz. (225ml); celery 8 fl.oz. (225ml).

Dandelion 14 fl.oz. (400ml).

Dandelion 8 fl.oz. (225ml); asparagus 4 fl.oz. (100ml).

Nettle 6 fl.oz. (175ml) a day.

Parsley 6 fl.oz. (175ml) a day mixed with another juice.

Pumpkin (or marrow) 1pt. (550ml).

Horseradish (grated) 4oz. (100g) with warm water.

Those with water retention should avoid added salt (sodium chloride) and not eat highly salted foods.

Worms (in gastric tract)

A remedy that removes worms is called an antihelmintic. The following are recognized. A two week course is advised, be sure that the stools are not able to be recycled into the environment:

Pumpkin 16 fl.oz. (450ml).

1 dessertspoonful garlic juice in 10 fl.oz. (275ml) warm water.

Wounds

To heal wounds, vitamins C & K and protein are needed. Vitamin K is found in Alfalfa, and protein in Comfrey. Therefore a good combination is:

Alfalfa 6 fl.oz. (175ml), comfrey 6 fl.oz. (175ml); carrot 4 fl.oz. (100ml).

CHAPTER 8

JUICES FOR PLEASURE

There must be a place in a therapeutic book such as this to consider the delights of raw juices as drinks in their own right. Some juices, such as pineapple, papaya, tomato, carrot, citrus, apple and beetroot, are delicious on their own. But, once you have a juicer, do spend some time experimenting with blends to suit you, your friends and family.

Try some of these and then work our your own.

BANANA FOAM Simmer teaspoonful of marjoram in $\frac{1}{2}$ cupful water for five minutes. Cool: put in blender with 2 skinned bananas, one egg white and a little crushed ice. Blend until frothy and then serve. (The same can be done with pineapple).

APRICOT-APPLE Take $\frac{1}{2}$ cupful of dried apricots and blend it with cupful apple juice and $\frac{1}{2}$ cupful of apple juice.

GINGER-APPLE-CHERRY Take a piece of ginger and blend it with a cupful apple juice and $\frac{1}{2}$ cupful cherry juice plus $\frac{1}{2}$ cupful ice.

PLUM-APPLE Stone three plums, add $\frac{1}{2}$ cupful plum juice. 1 cupful apple juice and 1 cupful ice. Blend and serve.

PINEAPPLE-GRAPE Blend together 1 cupful grapes without stones, 1 slice pineapple and 1 cupful ice with 1 tablespoonful honey.

GOURMET APERITIF One cupful tomato, $\frac{1}{3}$ cupful celery, $\frac{3}{8}$ cupful parsley, $\frac{1}{2}$ lemon, 1 cupful carrot, $\frac{1}{2}$ cupful ice, 1 teaspoonful sea salt. Mix and serve.

INDEX